heroes for hire

A TALL TALE OF THE CATSKILLS
(SUMMER OF 1969)

by

JOHN MARSHAL
Kincheloe

MOUNTAIN ARTS MEDIA

Published by Mountain Arts Media
Fleischmanns, NY

First Edition of 500 copies, 2018

ISBN: 978-0-692-18922-1

Book designed by Silvertop Graphics
New Kingston, NY

Acknowledgements

Heroes is a short book,
and so this will be a short list of people
to whom I owe a great deal.

THANKS TO:

David Krajicek—
for an early and helpful critique of the manuscript.

Mike and Joanne Finberg
who did the only real (and fantastic) editing of my final draft.

Bill Birns of Mountain Arts Media
and Lisa Tait of Silvertop Graphics
for believing in the book and making it come true.

Dennis Metnick, for legal advice and assistance.

Clarke Sanford—himself—
who enjoyed an early draft and offered some helpful advice.

Brother George's careful eye and lifelong companionship.

Nancy Carol, whose pictures of the farm grace many of these pages
and who was also gracious enough to add her talents
in designing the back cover.

Andy Van Benschoten, for his old and dear friendship
and tremendous assistance in the publishing aspect of things.

And lastly, my four wonderful children,
Lauren, Rachel, Jackson and Arleigh,
and my wife, Kate Darling,
who has somehow managed to put up with me
through both the darkest and brightest of days...

"Those who labor in the earth
are the chosen people of God,
if ever he had a chosen people...."

THOMAS JEFFERSON
Notes on the State of Virginia
1785

—————————

"Farts...."

ROLAND VAN BENSCHOTEN
New Kingston, New York
1969

For Kate...

chapter one

"I was born for a storm; calm does not suit me."
Andrew Jackson said that.

I was born in the middle of the day, in the middle of the week, in the middle of the month, in the middle of the year, in the middle of a century, more or less. Don't know if it was raining just then but it may have seemed like bad weather to Mother Kincheloe because there were two of us and the second baby (me) was a complete surprise. She named me John, which means "gift of God." My mother had a very complicated sense of humor.

This story is a Tall Tale about the Catskill Mountains of New York state, and perhaps such a yarn is best told by a person who shows up at the tail-end of a large family as a surprise. Someone who learns early the benefit of letting their voice be heard in a crowd even if they have to stretch things a little to get peoples' attention. Maybe it doesn't hurt either to get born right on top of somebody else. It gives you a head start on this 'love thy neighbor' business, which can be really valuable when telling stories about human beings, who, taken as a species, mostly make you want to throw up. My twin brother and I had been wrestling for space and or learning to get along with Mr. Neighbor in cramped quarters for a good nine months even before we came out, landing, as I mentioned, right in the middle of things.

Unlike most Tall Tales, this one is mostly true. At least as true as it can be for a story about things that happened so long ago.

Americans generally seem to love a story about larger than life events, and we haven't had a good one come out of these mountains since Washington Irving left us a couple of corkers a really long time ago. He was spinning tales about Dutch Poltroons, dead bowlers, and Headless Horsemen. And, of course, one other poor dumb fuck who fell asleep and took a nap that lasted a great deal longer than it should have.

This one is not about any of those things: it's about cows. Cows and two nineteen-year-old boys who woke up one morning on a Catskill dairy farm to find themselves looking at the beginning of the best summer of their lives. One that would lead them into many adventures: a world of backbreaking work they never imagined existed, true love, a fist fight of truly Homeric proportions, a close encounter with a legendary figure from America's Tallest Tale, the "beginning of a [more than one] beautiful friendship", the world's most intelligent dog and an accidental starring role in this country's first rock festival. The one people can't seem to stop talking about even now.

It is a Tall Tale about a special summer. One of those that just seem to come around now and then, where things fall into place and go the right way, at least most of the time. Take the rain for example. It is always raining in the Catskills, or at least it is often cloudy and about to rain. The Indians who lived here before the first Scottish and Dutch settlers called it "Land in the Clouds." But not that summer. The days were beautiful and it only rained at night, except for a day or two here and there, and as it turned out, our heroes certainly made the most of that. It was the summer of 1969.

My twin brother George and I came to the mountains to work as hired hands on the dairy farm of Roland Van Benschoten near the tiny village of New Kingston, New York. We had grown up playing Davy Crockett and Georgie Russell in Crafton, a small middle class "borough" on the western edge of Pittsburgh, Pennsylvania. We were happy there, killing imaginary Indians and Mexicans at every turn. With two older brothers and a sister, the small house was always busy and filled with love—at least when my big (and I mean Big) brother Bob wasn't trying to kill Larry, the middle boy, an activity he put a certain amount of quality time and effort into. Jane and Bob Sr. really were loving and devoted parents, even for the 1950's, but with that many children there was a lot of friction I suppose and being the youngest had its advantages. Easier to hide sometimes. One place we hid out in was the television room, especially Saturday mornings and weekend nights. Without the more modern distractions of video games, cell phones and computers in general, when the weather was bad it was either read, which we loved to do, play with "little men"—small plastic soldiers from every war ever fought on the planet—or watch the marvelous "wasteland" of fifties television. The family sitcoms were often amusing, if you didn't mind being embarrassed half to death when Princess listened in on Bud's private conversations creating endless problems for the Andersons on *Father Knows Best*. But the big lessons I learned came from the thousands of hours of TV westerns, like *Maverick* and *Have Gun will Travel*, and the heroic figures Errol Flynn, Gary Cooper, Jimmy Stewart and John Wayne usually played in the older movies the networks re-ran constantly back then trying to fill up air time. *The Adventures of Robin Hood, The Dawn Patrol, Stage Coach,*

The Spirit of St. Lewis, Captain Blood, Northwest Passage: these were all game changers. But when Walt Disney cast Fess Parker as the King of the Wild Frontier he hit an exposed nerve ending for a whole generation of little boys who couldn't stop dreaming of firing flintlocks in really tight situations.

George and I took these fantasies to new heights whenever we entered the woods next to our house. We were knights and frontiersmen and adventuring pirates and had pretty much fought the entire Civil War to a successful conclusion several times before puberty and 7th grade reared their ugly heads, and then our parents moved to Mount Lebanon, a big wealthy white-guy suburb south of the city. Once we got over being in a gigantic school surrounded by strangers—the goddamned junior high school had a thousand kids in it—things smoothed out. (There are a lot of girls to look at in a school that big.) Those long years of classes, sports and fledgling dating prepared us well enough for freshman year at the Ivy League colleges we landed in, but nobody in all that time had ever mentioned anything about being up close and personal with the ass end of a cow.

"Farming it" was my brother's idea. Actually, it was Andy Van Benschoten's idea. He was George's proctor at Harvard, which is a fancy name for the graduate student who buys beer for the freshmen entry under his charge. Andy wanted to go to Czechoslovakia that summer but his father, Roland, naturally wanted him to come home to the farm to help with the milking and the haying. Andy's elegant solution was to send the two of us instead—much in the manner that draftees hired substitutes in the Civil War to take their place amongst the grape and the canister.

A young Andy V. B. facing Stoughton Hall with University Hall and the statue of John Harvard looking over his shoulder from across the freshman 'Yard.' George thought he looked like Robert Culp when he first met him, which was pretty cool. How could you not like someone who reminded you of Hoby Gilman from *Track Down*?　　　Photo by Charlie Olchowski.

"Go ahead George, you'll love it there," he told him. "The work's fun and the girls are beautiful. Christ, they'll be all over a college jock like you. Take your brother. Boy, I wish I could be there to see it." he said.

Well, I went along. Our folks had moved to Detroit the same day we graduated from high school in Pittsburgh the year before. In fact, we came home from the ceremony surprised to find our house completely empty except for two traveling bags in the center of the living room floor. Graduation presents. Welcome home boys. Congratulations! Bye now. That first summer after high school was spent living out of those bags in various friends' basements in Pittsburgh. I didn't particularly want to try that again and after a year at college, sitting alone in the Motor City for a summer did not seem like such a good ticket either, so hell, why not? Might learn something.

We pulled into the Catskills on our nineteenth birthday, June 13th, 1969, on the heels of one of the worst summer storms anyone, even the old folks, could remember—a harbinger of something, no doubt. It was nothing to us. We were so hung over from the night before which we spent in Syracuse pounding Budweiser with a college friend of George's that we drove right through the town of New Kingston and didn't see it.[1] Well, we must have seen something I guess because about a mile past it I pulled our sister Margot's borrowed white Chevelle over to the side of the road and leaned my head on the steering wheel.

"What are you doing?" asked George.

"Resting," I said.

"Good," he said and laid his head on the shotgun window.

---

1. G. Kincheloe, At the Bishop's House: Recollections of a Night in Sacred Hell (Cambridge: Harvard University Press, 1973), 10-13. Welcome to the first footnote. If you read a lot of history like I do, one can grow rather fond of footnotes—you can discover some great stuff foraging around in them. The fact that you are reading this one shows that you still have a spark of childhood curiosity in you, and that maybe your computer and television haven't turned your brain to mush yet. (The Life of Riley, The Three Stooges, and Leave It To Beaver almost did that to mine long ago.) Anyway, neither of us had ever actually met Gerry Ward yet—the guy we stayed with and got wasted with that last night in civilization. His father, a Methodist Bishop, was a friend of our father, an American Baptist minister, and our older brothers had played football and roomed together at Harvard nine years before. These odd connections led to an immediate and depraved friendship. Fortunately, the Bishop and his wife were not home that night.

After a few minutes of this, I asked, "what do you think; was that a town?"

"A what?"

"Look," I said. "I think I saw a store—post office?... maybe a church on the left. I don't know."

So far our conversations all day had taken place on a need-to-know basis only. There was a brief nostalgic chat as we came down through Cooperstown from the New York State Thruway. This had been a nod to Mother Kincheloe's courageous decision to drive what must have been 100 miles out of her way to take us to the Baseball Hall of Fame as ten-year-olds. But our jog down memory lane had been more of a stumble—not much communication beyond a few well timed affirmative gestures and grunts. Now we both had our eyes closed and the words were coming out in slow bunches, like bad dialogue in a B minus horror movie directed by Roger Corman.

"A church, huh? Nope. No church; no church—nothing like that."

About that point it began to dawn on us that here we had come some five hundred miles from Michigan and had quite probably driven right through the place we had promised to spend the next two and a half months in and only vaguely noticed it.

"Well, I guess you better turn this thing around and go back for a look," George said after a while. So we did.

It was New Kingston alright and it wasn't much bigger on the second drive through, but after a sober-up soda on the front steps of the little country store/post office in the middle of the village, we found the turn off for the farm about a half a mile down on the right, and drove across a plank bridge and up a winding dirt road lined on either side with giant

The Van Benschoten farm as seen from the New Kingston road.

trees. There was a huge faded-white barn ahead on the left and beyond it the old white farmhouse surrounded by more big trees. The first thing you would notice about the Van Benschoten farm on a June afternoon is that it may be one of the prettiest places on earth. For us, even through our haze, it was like entering an alternate universe with lush green hay fields rolling away on either side and deep woods climbing away past the house into the mountains above. There were beautiful flowers everywhere and a huge vegetable garden on the right side beyond the barn just before the driveway went over a small creek and curled behind the house.

We pulled the car halfway around that drive and cut the engine in front of some garage-like sheds. I remember a moment of panic sitting there getting ready to stick our faces into something we did not belong to in any sense of the word and realizing for the first time that day how bad we really might look and smell to some strict old farmer, but just then Andy's father came out of the house and one look at him told me we were going to be fine.

Roland Van Benschoten looked like a sawed-off weather-ized version of John Wayne dressed in an old white v-neck tee shirt, an ample belly protruding slightly over sagging jeans. With massive rounded shoulders on a thick frame, and big meaty fists at the end of huge arms—everything about him spelled work of the every-day-all-your-life variety. That should have been frightening, but the guy had this big disarming smile under a shock of swept back whitish hair and I swear his eyes were twinkling as he looked us over.

"Have a hard drive, did ya?" he said laughing at the two of us. "We had a terrific storm here last night, afraid we might of lost you boys in it. Awful weather. Welcome to the Catskills. I'm Roland."

Faye Van Benschoten, Roland's wife, came slowly out of the kitchen door. I have come to love this woman dearly but at that moment I got the uncomfortable impression we were being stalked. In contrast to Roland, Faye was a small thin creature with darting eyes behind horn-rimmed glasses, wispy blonde hair and prominent teeth. No smile just yet. I don't even remember what she said but the look on her face was distinctly one of 'what has God done to me now'? Who could blame her? We learned later that what Faye really needed that June day was a new kitchen oven to replace the one that had just blown up and one good steady farm hand who knew what he was doing around cows and who wouldn't upset the status quo. Instead she had two city kids who didn't know anything about work on a farm, were probably going to be a lot of trouble and the cost of the second one was sending the Sears Catalogue picture of her new range winging away into the distant future. Besides, they looked drunk.

The first view you get of the farmhouse when you drive in.
The side on the left used to be the "front,"
at least back when you rode in on a wagon.

Well, God bless Faye anyway...she took us into the house. The inside of the V.B. home was a shock; lots of rooms—a kitchen, living room to the right of a hallway, stairs going up with a beautiful old wooden banister on the left side. The house was nearly one hundred years old; it was nicely furnished and smelled like cow shit. Let's get this squared away. I don't know what I was expecting, but too many *Lassie* episodes had evidently prepared me to assume that an old farm house would feel and smell like my grandmother's place in West Virginia—snug, elderly perhaps. Let's just take the cookies out of the oven and give 'em a small preview shall we? Well, even old Clara Kincheloe's dear departed in-laws in Mosby's Confederate Rangers (the ones that weren't farmers) might have hesitated in the face of this overwhelming odor.

The living fact of cow was everywhere. I was disoriented enough as it was and I damn near bolted back outside into the fresh air. Instead I put my chin down on my chest, slowly wagged my head from side to side and waited for the fear to subside. If the situation hadn't been so desperate and surreal my brother and I might have dissolved into a killing zone of hysterical giggling. (The kind of crazed laughter you try to hold off but can't. The kind in which you might lose all self-control at a Baptist Youth Fellowship meeting on a tired Sunday night watching a slide show about missionaries. There's no way out and you and the orphan wonder, Ernie Dunn, are fighting back tears because, thanks to an accidental camera angle, the guy with the hose watering the front lawn of the church school in East Bethlehem, Malaysia for the last three slides appears to be taking a piss of elephantine proportions.)

We didn't laugh. Instead I slowly looked up at George the way Christ must have looked up at Peter at the crack of dawn on Good Friday. It was a profoundly searching unspoken inquiry filled with accusations of betrayal, sorrow and fear—a look that should have melted his heart. Evidently not wishing to tamper with holy precedent, George looked away. [2]

---

2. There was a Baptist Orphanage in Pittsburgh (back in the days when there were still white kids nobody wanted) that funneled children into our Sunday school and youth groups. My minister dad worked in the Council of Churches so he rarely preached in the churches we went to, but as members of a religiously oriented family, we spent a LOT of time in those achingly somber situations. Any distraction was welcome and Orphan Ernie earned my lasting admiration many times over. Imagine a fat twelve-year-old with a big square head suddenly rearing up and firing a huge rubber band point-blank across a table at a substitute Sunday School teacher who is reading out loud, and then appear, in the very next instant, as the one kid in the group who could not possibly have done it. One night in BYF they told us to turn to the back of the hymnal and sing *How Great Thou Art* which was pasted on the inside of the back cover. Well, Ernie's copy only had the words: "Property of Mount Lebanon Baptist Church" stamped on it there. And so that's what he sang over and over again at the top of his lungs, for the next three or four minutes. Since George and I were sharing the hymnal with him, we joined right in.

chapter two

And then an angel appeared.

"Boys," said Faye, "I'd like you to meet our niece, Claire. She lives just across the road."

Tall, blond, beautiful—she was everything an earnest wannabe farm hand could have dreamed of and more. I clearly remember thinking: "What smell?" We had in fact just gone back outside into the yard to get our bags when she appeared along with Andy's younger sister, Mary Ann, called Wee-wee (no kidding) who was also a wonderful surprise. They were nice enough to us, although they both told me later that their first impression was that we looked like morons in our college-boy-tight-jeans-no-socks-penny-loafer-madras-shirt outfits. And then they were gone. But a tide had turned and the summer ahead was suddenly filled with sweet promises.

"Can't hay it in those shoes boys; they'll have to go," Roland said first thing the next morning and took us into Margaretville, the nearest real town to the tiny village of New Kingston, to get us outfitted. On the second floor of a general store on Main Street named Bussy's, (which seemed like a place we could have bought supplies on our way to fight in the Civil War), we found what we needed, which wasn't much—a good pair of work boots, a straw cowboy hat for the sun, and a couple of pairs of 'Boss of the Road' dungarees. I employ the 'd' word because these were not regular Levis but thinner denim work pants with side pockets on one leg and a hammer loop on the other. They were just the thing for hot work, which we soon learned was exactly what farmin' it was all about. Rol (pronounced Rawl), as everyone called him, took us back to the farm and introduced us to the tools of his trade: the barn where about 40 cows needed to be milked twice a day, the milk room, just inside and to the right of the big doors you entered from the house side of the barn, where a giant aluminum tank held the fresh milk and all the milking equipment was washed and stored, and best of all—the tractors.

These were two big orange beauties made by Allis Chalmers. One seemed fairly new, the other ancient, with a braking system consisting of two big levers on either side of the seat that you had to grab a hold of and pull back on if you wanted to stop it.

"You're shitting us here aren't you Roland?" George asked about those brakes.

"Nope boys. You'll get the hang of it soon enough. When you need to brake you just steer with your knees, or you can grow another arm real quick-like. Your choice."

Rol chuckled softly when he said things like that. His laughter when working in the barn or fields was something like a series of wild snorts, but at meals or sitting in the living room in his favorite chair, the big guy's laughter was bizarre and contagious. Actually saying the words, "Ha! Ha! Ha!," his whole body would shake and his face contort; his voice would go way up high and tears would form. It's one of the best sounds I've ever heard. He went out of his way those first few days to be patient and gentle with us, probably sensing how completely baffled and ignorant we were about everything he was teaching us. That included how to prepare a cow for milking by wiping her udder with a wet rag, how to hook up the milking machines to the beasts without getting stomped, when to take them off, how to set up the apparatus that carried the milk from a central container through a system of clear hoses back to the refrigerated tank in the milk room, and how to keep everything in there shiny and germ free by careful washing. We learned about servicing the tractors and other haying machinery—an essential task every morning after breakfast which included pumping grease into all kinds of strange places. I had never even seen a grease gun before. Soon enough it was out into the fields, all morning and all afternoon learning how to run several different kinds of equipment and then back for another round of milking, a task which seemed so complicated and intense at first that time seemed to stand still while you were in that vast ancient barn.

Roland did everything slowly, even breathing. Patiently, rather; there was no hurry up in the man. Instead of creating frustration in my nineteen-year-old brain, however, a feeling akin to serenity flowed out of his work pace. I suppose if you raced around a farm trying to get things done in a hurry it would kill you or drive you and others working with you insane in a couple of years. Just a theory, but if Roland's presence hadn't been such a calming influence who knows what we might have done. I remember that first week as a kind of daze...working all day, and (have you ever done this?) dreaming of work all night. Being so exhausted by the time dinner was over that ten minutes of a Mets game in front of the TV in the living room would do it nicely. Then up to bed and sound asleep until Rolly (that was his other nickname) would be waking one of us with his big gentle voice for the early milking. Faye would help in the barn every morning with the chores allowing one of us to sleep in. Without that break in the routine, I believe there would have been a twin suicide.[3]

Yes, old Rol broke us in easy. We had both been learning to drive the tractors, (which by the way is the greatest fucking kid-dream-come-true thing in the world if you've never done it before) for several days before he took us aside one morning and quietly mentioned that the older Allis Chalmers had a nasty habit of slipping out of gear once in a while.

"Probably won't happen boys, but if it does—hang on."

Of course it did happen. It happened one morning as George was coming down Miller Road, a steep dirt side road you took to get to one of the hay fields on the other side of the New Kingston road from the barn and house. He had the hay rake on the back when she popped, just to give the whole thing some extra gravity, and he came flying out into the middle of that main road unannounced, pulling hard on the wheel to the right and just barely managing to avoid dumping the entire outfit into the river on the other side. No one was coming along just then, but George damn near browned up his new Boss of the Road work pants.

---

3. Which could have been kind of cool in its own twisted way. We might have made the front page of the *New York Daily News*, which had become our only (and ridiculously sensational) link to the outside world. That summer was just jammed full of amazing news stories which The News did its utmost to exploit on every possible level. If you have ever seen a New York City tabloid at work you can imagine how gleefully their giant headlines reported the Sharon Tate murders. Chappaquiddick anyone? We had grown up reading *The Pittsburgh Press* and the *Pittsburgh Post Gazette*, fairly normal big city newspapers, and had no idea that whacko right wing editors could have so much fun splashing people's personal nightmares all over their front page in letters four inches high. Every day seemed to bring some new horror.

"Jesus Christ, Roland," he said when he drove up to us later in another field.

"Well son, that's what the brakes are for," Roland said, laughing. Hard to argue with that.

I haven't mentioned the rest of the immediate farm family yet. Besides the lovely Mary Ann, in early high school and spending most of her time with friends hiding, perhaps, from the new farm hands, there were two lucky house cats, two dogs—one retired—and Gram. We met Gram at supper the first night. She was Roland's mother, eighty years old, tiny and frail-looking and a source of major amusement in the dining room for every meal. That first night she won my heart by suddenly jumping up from her place near the end of the table, leaning as far out over it as she could and grabbing the mashed potatoes.

"Pardon my boardinghouse reach!" she triumphantly exclaimed. Laura (her name from before she was Gram) was everybody's favorite. Between meals she could most often be found in the living room napping on the couch under an old knitted red and black blanket.[4] Gram was simply the best. Probably because she didn't have to teach us anything or put up with our great ignorance about all things on the farm, she quickly welcomed us as an amusing distraction (for her) and loved us seemingly without reservation.

George had the good sense to realize that we needed to show her, in our own alien suburban way, how much we appreciated this attitude. Sometime during that first week

---

4. In the routine that developed we would have about a fifteen minute break every day after lunch and it became a race between George and myself to see who could leave the dining room table first and get to the fabled "Gram blanket" on the couch. I swear to you it had the magical quality of granting instant sleep to anyone who touched it.

This is Gram just as she looked in the summer of '69, except for the old fashioned outfit. It was her mother's wedding dress and she wore this for one of the New Kingston Whoop-de-doos, a bizarre concept I will explain later.

he decided the best way to do it would be to surprise her with a personal touch—a letter to the little local paper she loved to read. "The Catskill Mountain News" came out once a week in Margaretville on Wednesdays carrying news and chewy gossip about who had visited who on the nearby farms near the smaller villages like New Kingston, Andes and Bovina. It took us the better part of a day throwing ideas back and forth as we passed each other at work. The finished product, which to our delight was printed the very next week, read like this:

> Dear News,
> The sunshine in the New Kingston Valley
> seems just a little brighter today as
> The Roland Van Benschoten family has been joined by
> "heroes for hire" from the big city, George and
> John Kincheloe.
> Both are for Gram.
> Rufus Van Benschoten

Gram loved it. Especially the fact that the letter was signed by Rufus, Roland's prize cow dog, who Gram admired. Rufus was a big gray and white Australian Shepard with eyes so strange we thought at first maybe a human being was trapped inside. In fact George was pretty sure Che Guevara, the handsome Argentine revolutionary who was Fidel's buddy, had been reincarnated right there in New Kingston. I agreed that the idea had merit, but we did the math and the CIA (okay, their Bolivian hit men in training) had not quite yet filled Che full of holes when Rufus was born. Close, though. That dog was talented with cows and certainly smarter than me; he proved this to everyone's satisfaction a couple of times that summer.

A cow dog's main job was to push the herd into the barn for milking twice a day which seemed fairly easy because, as far as I could tell, those cows wanted to get in the barn as fast as possible anyway to get rid of all that milk they were lugging around. These big critters all had individual names like Flo and Peanut and Big Red and Ginger (she was an asshole) and knew exactly where their individual stall was located and would walk right into them on their own. Usually. As they came in Rufus would run around the barn hassling them for fun and then plop himself into a big wheel barrow near the door and sit there contentedly while he watched us work for a couple of hours. It occurred to me right away that the dog considered himself somewhat superior to the humans he worked with and observed daily, and there was some terrific evidence all around to support this theory even if the reincarnation one didn't work out.

Rufus also had a refined sense of humor which nearly got me killed twice, but I'll get back to that. Bobby Sox was the other dog. She was black with white paws, smaller and fatter than her replacement but had been an excellent cow mover in her day according to the Boss. Bobby, now retired due to failing vision and what seemed like brain damage, spent her days doing what we quickly dubbed orbits: a slow intense shuffle in the middle of the drive that went around the big white farmhouse. It became a comforting feature of life on the farm to know that Bobby Sox, aka "the Bear," was on some kind of eternal patrol circling the house, looking out for the rest of us.

The big barn where the milking got done was a universe unto itself and it was only after my first few visits there that the inside of the house began to smell alright to me. Look. A cow has two functions in the barn: to unload milk and take huge dumps which fall into a manure trough conveyor belt thing behind them. At the touch of a switch this belt carries their excrement around the barn and out the back door to a manure spreader which, of course, later spreads this stuff in the fields to make the hay and grass grow for the cows to ingest so they can come back in every day and do it again. No part of this smells good while it is happening. I forgot to mention that the other thing they do in the barn is eat. But they do this everywhere else they go as well. All day.

I have no idea how people did this milking and moving of shit in a barn before electricity without murder and suicide on a daily basis. But the keynote here is that the barn smelled like, well, a barn, and the difference between this over-powering stench and the memory of what the Mount Lebanon swimming pool had smelled like (where we had been substitute life guards the summer before) was notable. I mentioned this discrepancy just once to George but the look in his eye made me decide to drop the subject forever.

One of the great sideshows while you were milking was the daily soap opera of the barn cats. Farmers keep cats in their barns to wipe out any rodent population which could threaten the well-being of everything I suppose, if they got into the grain in the silos or the stored hay or the milking equipment. It was anybody's guess how many cats lived in there. Roland had no idea; he said the number varied almost from week to week as new ones were born and others drifted off for personal reasons. He had names for some of the veterans and evidently enjoyed watching to see who was calling whose bluff (who was top kick of the commune) any given week. He also made sure they had food and would occasionally pour out some fresh milk for a delighted crowd that would appear out of nowhere when it heard the right audio clues. They were scruffy independent critters and a source of amusement with their cat antics. Once in a long while, legend had it, one of them would be in a magic place at a predestined moment and get adopted into the family up to the "Big House." As I said, there were two "lucky ones" that summer living inside and like any other pampered house cats, acted as if that world revolved around them. I noticed they didn't go out much, and certainly never strayed anywhere near the barn. No doubt harboring memories of the raucous world they had miraculously escaped from, they had no wish to associate with that sort of riff raff ever again.

We had only been with the V.B.'s a matter of days when the first Sunday arrived. There is no "weekend" on a dairy farm—just Sunday. And of course the goddamned cows have to be milked even on that day because the Maker of the Universe forgot to mention anything about a day of rest to them, but other than that work pretty much stops. George and I needed sleep and time off too much to accept Gram's offer of church that morning but I agreed to take a Sunday afternoon drive with her and Rolly and Faye to make up for our heathenish sloth. I only did it once, but as Tom Rush sang many times from the record player in our bedroom that summer: "no regrets."

Gram and I sat in the back seat of the family car while Roland drove the four of us around the valley from farm to farm. I had never been for a ride in a car traveling at that velocity before. Roland's idea of cruising speed was about as fast as a tractor goes when you are really flying on one, which is to say 20-25 miles an hour. On a tractor that's fast—even scary—but I kept looking over my shoulder thinking we would all be killed any second by some innocent yahoo going 50 or 60 miles-an-hour around a bend behind us.

"What's the matter son?" Gram eventually asked.

"Nothing, nothing Gram," I answered. "I guess my neck is just a little stiff from all this milking business."

Turns out, the object of the drive was to inspect everybody else's hay fields and herds and Roland and Faye discussed some aspect of each one as we went by. Most of what they said didn't even make sense to me at the time. But the one thing I remember clearly, other than the constant fear of being creamed from behind, was when Gram spied the first herd we went by.

"Cows," she muttered in disgust. "First cows I've seen all day....Cows!"

Later that afternoon I attended the first class meeting of "Cattle 307: Hazards of the Dairy Barn." Here's what I learned: only an idiot walks into a barn in shorts and bare feet. I think it was Faye who said, "Doc Fairbairn's down to the barn, John. Go see what he's up to. You might find it interesting." Interesting? What I was a party to for the next hour was something I would never have believed possible. Doc was a tall thin (but powerful) balding young veterinarian—I guessed right out of the Navy based on his colorful language.[5] He had been called in because a cow was having trouble giving birth. It had never occurred to me that a cow

---

5. That guess was based on an encounter in Lake Geneva, Wisconsin three summers earlier with our cousin Bill Bradley, who visited us for a few hours at a Council of Churches camp where we were working as dishwashers. Until then I thought the Boy Scouts did a fine job of teaching me how to use profanity, but Billy's constant and imaginative employment of the "f" word as subject, verb, adverb, adjective, pronoun and dangling participle, often all in the same sentence, was truly awesome. He had just completed eight weeks of basic training at the Great Lakes Naval Station where he had been studying at the feet of the masters.

would need help doing something like that but it had also never occurred to me that I would ever see a man put on a long plastic glove and stick his whole arm up a cow's ass.

Whoa. I imagine I looked like a cartoon version of a city boy—eyes wide, jaw gaping—but the vet didn't stop to laugh at me; he was too pissed off at the cow in front of him.

"Fuck you four thousand fucking ways, you fucking miserable piece of fucking shit." Or words very much to that effect. He turned to me.

"Come over here whoever you are, I need some fucking help."

Seems our young mother to be had managed to get her baby turned around in some awkward position and then decided, as only a cow can do, that whatever was going on back there wasn't as important as eating. She had quit pushing.

"You mean she's not helping?" I asked innocently.

"Fuck no. Here, grab this and pull."

With that the Doc whipped out a giant hook on the end of a large shiny chain, reached back into the place where baby cows come from, all the way up to his shoulder, and evidently attached it to the calf.

"If we don't do this they'll both probably die. Let's try to pull it out."

So we did. Both of us pulled with everything we had, sweating and cursing and getting nowhere. Mom may have changed her mind and been trying to help—who knows— because suddenly there was cow shit spraying all around us. I can't say for sure what the good Doctor yelled at that moment but the man was an artist. We both stepped back and looked at each other.

"Don't worry about that," he said. "We can't stop now."

And so we pulled some more. And just when I thought I couldn't take it any longer several things happened at once: the baby calf suddenly came flying out in a shower of God-knows-what and the big cow gave a loud bellow and slipped in the awful muck she had created and her hoof went down into the manure trough landing on top of my bare right foot.

'Shit. I'm crippled,' was my first thought.

"Damn you all to hell you miserable bitch," Doctor Fairbairn said quietly. "It's a bull."

I don't know what was worse: my pain or his grief. You see, all that effort is more than worth it if the calf is a heifer, a female, a future milk-maker. But a boy? Sell it for veal after a month or two, no big deal. Of course none of that made any sense to me at that moment. Nothing mattered except whether or not my foot was broken into a thousand pieces.

"Thanks a lot, son. You ought to get some shoes on."

"You're right," I said, "and you're welcome." I limped out of there knowing that I was not in Mount Lebanon anymore and could never go back, at least not as the same person. I had seen too much.

chapter three

Well, it turns out my mangled foot wasn't broken after all, just mangled a bit, and other than the injury to my pride, as in: how could you be so stupid as to wander into a barn without work boots on?, the shock of witnessing the not so immaculate birth wore off quickly. After a few days of sorting out the field equipment and learning the mysteries of the barn, Roland must have figured we were ready to get down to the real business at hand. One evening at supper, with a fierce gleam in his eyes, he announced: "Boys, tomorrow we'll start hayin' it." Hayin' it is what summer on the farm is all about. If you can get a significant amount of hay from the fields into the barn in those magical weeks between the middle of June and the end of August, then your year is going to be a good one. Sounds simple. It wasn't.

Now days farmers have big modern machines that take newly-cut hay and turn it into giant rolls only another giant machine can move around. These monsters get covered in white plastic and left out in the fields until needed. In 1969 you had to bale hay, and each bale, a twenty to thirty pound rectangular chunk of compacted dead grass held together with two strips of tight twine, had to be moved individually to a safe harbor in the barn. And that was just the very end of a very complicated process.

It went like this: Roland would choose the field, attacking it with his little gray Ford tractor that held a cutting bar off to one side and, driving in careful circles, mow the grass down. After a day or two that new-cut grass (depending on

moisture levels and God knows what else), would have to
be "conditioned." This became my job many mornings and
it entailed hitching the conditioner—a big ugly mother with
huge rubber rollers—behind one of the Allis Chalmers and
making sure the whole field got sucked through the rolls.
I'm still not sure what the point was, something about breaking the individual stalks, but it had to be done and of course
driving a tractor anywhere is fun so I never complained.

The next step was more interesting to watch. "Tedding"
the hay meant running yet another strange looking machine
over the field, but a tedder had small metal parts on it that
picked the grass up and threw it around. The Boss had two
of these and the older one was so ancient it was mostly built
out of wood and had little tiny claws that grabbed the hay
and worried it like a chattering alien insect. Noisy as hell
and fun to see angry. Then, if it hadn't rained yet, the hay
would be raked into long rows for the baler to come by and
suck up and turn into bales.

Obviously you have to know exactly what you are doing
to keep all of that equipment working for you at the same
time in different places for maximum effect, and our new
employer was superb at it. It doesn't take a genius to drag
any of those old beaters around behind a tractor, and so the
foot soldiers were in place, but Roland was the consummate
general running the campaign. Every morning he knew as if
by deep instinct which one of us should take what to where.
After breakfast, while gassing up and greasing up the tractors and their accessories next to the old garage by the big
house, he would assign us different weapons of choice to
take to specific far flung fields to fight the good fight against
time and the weather, and we would carefully hook them
up and be off.

I became the conditioning expert. Possibly the Boss saw a hint of perseverance in me I was unaware of, because what that called for was 1) staying awake and 2) having the patience to crawl under that cocksucking machine (sorry Gram) and take a knife and cut through the tightly wound grass strands that would jam the rollers every so often if the hay was still just the tiniest bit wet from the morning dew. Both of us ran the tedding equipment, but George became the expert raker; again, old Rol saw something there he liked. Raking the hay so that the baling can be done easily is a learned science, and George somehow became very good at it in a short time.

I mention staying awake. This was a formidable task some mornings, especially after the kind of nights we began to put in after that first week of seasoning. One of the scariest moments I had all summer was dozing off while conditioning and running the tractor too close to the low hanging branches of the only tree in the middle of the field I was working. Could have killed me, but the only thing that damn tree did was snatch off the straw cowboy hat I had proudly purchased at Bussy's and pitch it straight back into the conditioner's smiling maw. That hat was never the same and I was scared so shitless that I (almost) never fell asleep again while working, at least not while sitting way up on one of those funky tractor seats between those giant life-sucking tires.

Roland was kind enough to mention early on that it only took a second to die on a tractor. One tire dropping into one hidden woodchuck hole on the side of a hill and you could be under the tractor and gone.

"It's happened to a lot of good men who have done this all their lives" he said. I believed him. On a steep slope, George and I would both go real slow and sit up on the tire shield poised for at least an attempt to jump clear. Of course the danger of farming on hilly land as opposed to the numbing flatness of Kansas or Nebraska, for example, made it seem like more fun. At least when you are nineteen and stupid.

The Boss ran the baler and he was a magician, not only operating it flawlessly but constantly repairing it in the field. It is immutably fixed in the nature of a hay baling machine to break down at least once a day, maybe twice, and if you have ever seen one in action you would understand that they come by that kind of crankiness honestly. Baling was done after lunch in the full heat of the day with the hay in that particular field in just the right frame of mind and when Roland went to "balin' it" the fever was on him full throttle. He would go and go. No matter where you were on the farm in the afternoon if it was still, you could hear the sound of Rolly's tractor grinding away in the distance. That meant plenty of hay bales, and those bales needed to be picked up.

And that's how we met John V. B. and Guzzy. Young John Van Benschoten was usually called "John V.B."—who knows why—there were plenty of Van Benschotens around but only one who got the short initial treatment. John was Andy's cousin, Roland's nephew, (and, of course, Claire's brother!) who lived just across the road at the end of the farm driveway. He was tall and lanky with wispy light brown hair already beginning to recede a touch. He was also softspoken, articulate, and easygoing with a great smile thrown in as a bonus feature. So much for the country rednecks some asshole in Boston had warned us about. I think the smile came naturally because he spent a lot of time with Guzzy and it's impossible not to smile around Guzzy.

Guzzy's real name, we were told, was Butch, which wasn't exactly true—it is Paul—but it was about all you needed to hear to realize that you were in the presence of a guy who had already established himself as a living legend in this part of the Catskills at the tender age of eighteen or nineteen. Blonde, he stood about 5'8 or 9—a bit shorter than George and me—but built like one of those half-man-half-gods the Greeks were high on. And I mean the kind that could throw bulls and lions and minotaurs around all day. Guzzy didn't say much but you didn't want to miss it when he did.

"Well, what do we have here?" was probably the first thing he said to us and instead of being put off by those words, I was delighted. The sparkle—no other word will do—in his eyes let you know two things: the idea of city boys working with Roland was going to be a great source of amusement to him, but it was also going to be okay. Instead of coming off like Big Foot Mason, the archetypal frontier bully from Walt Disney's Davy Crockett movie, you could tell immediately that Guz didn't have a mean bone anywhere in that hulking farm-boy body.

We were first introduced to these two stalwarts the day after the Boss' haying announcement. Coming out of the fields for lunch, we found them perched on some ladders up against the side of the house near the little porch in the back that led into the kitchen.[6] Roland had hired them to paint the farmhouse that summer. The beauty of this arrangement was that once he had them there, (and anytime during the

---

6. This was, by the way, the only entrance to the house we ever used until years later. If you were working, as everyone always was, you stopped on the porch and took off your work boots and left them out there before you went in. There is an obvious reason for that and I will not insult the reader's intelligence with a further explanation.

Note: you can only get away with rambling on like this in a footnote, which is what makes them so useful.

morning that they showed up seemed to be okay) he had a haying team assembled. It only takes one person to run a tractor around a hay field that is getting prepped one way or another, but to pick up bales back then you really needed four bodies, preferably young, strong and able to work hard under tough conditions while getting along.

"Boys," Rolly said to us laughing, "these are your new haying partners. Try not to hurt each other. Let's eat."

Roland and Faye in the dining room circa 1969.
(It took a long time for her to smile at us this way.)

chapter four

Lunch was the best. Every meal at the farm was a serious occasion, if only because of the sheer amount of food on the table , but I loved the idea that lunch was designed to get a man, and I mean a BIG man, through the rest of a hard day's work. I had never been anywhere where they served mountains of hot mashed potatoes and gravy and roast beef (and hot fresh vegetables and bread and butter and jams and more vegetables and fruit and more mashed spuds) almost everyday for lunch. It is said around some holidays that tables can be "groaning" with the amount of food on them. Faye's tables didn't just groan; they sagged under the weight and wept.

Sounds too good to be true, and yes, there was a catch. Because Faye's oven was broken she had to cook all summer using only the top burners, which translated into only one way of cooking the beef. In the interest of self preservation I never asked how she did it, but the meat came out the same every meal—tasty but a little tough and cooked right through. After a week or two we learned that we were eating Daisy, a dairy cow who never performed up to expectations and wound up in the freezer. (Dairy cattle are not bred to taste good, just to make milk). George and I took to referring to our daily helpings of Daisy as "burned ass of cow." But only to each other.

The conversation around the table at any given meal could be memorable. Roland loved to laugh at a good story and Faye was a great storyteller; she seemed to know everything about everybody living or dead in the three or four closest villages to New Kingston—Margaretville, Andes, Bovina and Bovina Center. It was never malicious gossip, just what people had once said or were thinking about current events. Some of her stories were about growing up in a time when rural electricity and even tractors were fairly new. Roland mentioned once at lunch that they had gone back to using horses rather than tractors during World War II because gas was so scarce. He seemed wistful about it. Mary Ann told me later that her dad really loved horses—a trait she inherited. There were two of them living in the barn that she took care of. Maybe insurance in case we ever ran out of gasoline again, I don't know.

One of Faye's dining room beauties that I remember concerned a minister in Andes when she was a girl. She was talking to two friends and one of them remarked that the man had been practicing his sermons in the graveyard. The other said casually that "it would be the only time he ever had a full house." Roland would sometimes talk about going to dances when they were young and the wild things he and his two brothers had done on late night sprees before the daily grind of farm work and general adulthood had slowed his life down to the pace that ended his evenings dozing in front of the television. Of course it was a mistake to mention anything like that around us.

All in all, the company was delightful and the food was amazing. Faye came to the table one day with a miraculous combination of tomatoes and onions and who knows what else and everybody was saying how great it tasted.

"It's a good way to use up things you have," she said with typical modesty. "It's from a recipe in the Sunday *New York Times*. They've got this terrific cookbook they're offering. If I wasn't so Scottish, I'd send for one."

Gram would sit next to the end of the table near the kitchen which gave you a view of the big windows that faced out towards the barn and the driveway and the open fields. I'm guessing she had been sitting in that exact seat since her husband Andrew's mother had died. And that woman, Mary Van Benschoten, was the daughter of the guy who shot the sheriff during the Catskill Anti-Rent War of the 1840's and nearly got hung for it.[7] Gram was an institution, lending her own special observations and charm to every meal. I think the truest thing I ever heard anybody say came from her lips

---

7. This might end up being the only real footnote in this book, but I won't trouble you with all the historical details, fascinating as they are. Suffice it to say that most farmers in the Catskills in the mid 1800's did not own the land they worked and lived on, but rented it from wealthy absentee landowners whose families had been given large land grants back in colonial days. Of course this sucked and led to a lot of frustration and anger. At one point, many men got so bitter that they began dressing up like Indians and carrying guns and meeting to talk about how they were going to fix things. An asshole sheriff by the name of Osman Steel arrested some farmers and treated them badly, even leaving them freezing in an open wagon while he boozed it up in a tavern. Eventually he showed up at the wrong place and time bullying and bragging about "lead not penetrating steel." When he started to hurt somebody Roland's great grandfather blew him away. For this, he was hunted like a dog (people here still can show you places he hid), eventually jailed and sentenced to hang. Faye had an actual letter he wrote from prison talking passionately about his impending death, which is really cool to read, but they pardoned him when things calmed down and he married and lived a long quiet life. Andy, the guy who started all of this for us in 1969, is quite proud of his illustrious ancestor.

at that table one morning, but it takes a little background information to appreciate. You see, George rather quickly became romantically involved with the beautiful Claire, and they were together whenever she came home from Poughkeepsie where she was attending nursing school.

There is an old Catskill saying that your corn should be "knee high by the fourth of July." Well, ours was and George celebrated by kissing Claire for the first time in the hayloft on that splendid national holiday. For some reason I'll never know it delighted Gram that her granddaughter and my brother fell for each other. Not everybody was amused. Claire's father Jerry, who had built the house just across the road, was a truck driver and he never had any use for either of us. It didn't help matters that Claire already had a boyfriend, Mike Kapitko, whose natural love for and way with all things mechanical endeared him to Jerry. But Mike (who everyone referred to as "Stinky") was out at sea crawling around inside giant engines as a merchant marine, leaving the field open, or unattended, so to speak. I think Jerry lay awake at night praying for our deaths beneath the tractors.[8]

---

8. To be fair, I shouldn't be so hard on Jerry. I found out later that in his own way he was just as sharp as his two brothers and their father, Andrew, who had graduated from Cornell before taking over the family farm. Jerry had served in WWII (the Big One) and had driven trucks on the dangerous Red Ball Express route between the Normandy Beachhead and wherever the front was. Speaking fluent French (learned in high school!) he was a great favorite among his army buddies Over There for his ability to communicate with the locals—a priceless talent. One of his best friends was killed in France and Jerry became close to that young man's family in the states after the war. Obviously a fascinating guy; his affection for his future son in law being what it was at the time, my guess is he just didn't see anything in us worth befriending.

There is something else I may as well confess now, although if you've gotten this far you are not reading this thing for the dirty parts. I was still technically a virgin at that point and, unfortunately, this otherwise magic summer wasn't going to change that. There was one promising "date"—a sad adventure I'll tell you about later—but George seemed to have women coming out of the 1878 woodwork of that place. He even had two different girls visit him right there in remote New Kingston although I still don't know how they found us. One was a beautiful young woman named Becky Hartman. We first met her when we were twelve at Conference Point Camp on Lake Geneva, Wisconsin where every June our parents attended a week-long meeting of executives of the Council of Churches from cities all over the country.

Conference Point was an amazing place. All the Kincheloe children worked there on the staff as they reached the magic age of sixteen, for at least a summer. We spent two high school summers there washing dishes for up to five hundred people per meal and living with a bizarre and hilarious group of guys our age including Jeff (Beever) Davis and Tim (Mahatma) Meyers who are still crazy and who we still remain close to. It was a paradise of two teenage girls for every boy (on the staff), a big clear lake to swim in, and a lot of free time. One of the many things we learned to do there besides kiss pretty well and sneak around at night—there was a nearby water tower that a select group of "commandos" just had to climb—was to take advantage of the huge athletic field down by the lake that would flood briefly after a big thunderstorm leaving long puddles in the center. A good running start and you could go into a baseball slide and really fly, forty or fifty feet at a time.

Anyway, I had been in love with Becky for seven years at
that point, but somehow my brother had won her heart, or
at least her attention. When Gram found out some strange
girl was coming to see George she was more upset than I
ever saw her. As I walked into the dining room for breakfast
that morning she was standing at the far end of the table
by the window scowling as only an 80-year-old woman can
scowl.

"Complications!" she said loudly. "There are always complications!"

God bless that woman for sorting out one of the secrets
of the universe for me. Becky's visit certainly caused rather
astounding complications, but more on that by and by.

At the end of our first week an event occurred that can
only be called a "turning point." The day we met John V.B.
and Guzzy, John mentioned innocently enough that he and
Guz were graduating from high school that evening and
there just might be a party later; would we like to come
along?

Sure. Waugh.[9]

We went to the graduation and it was a tiny affair com-
pared to the one we had suffered through a year before in

---

9. Pronounced: whaaahh. Hell, there is no equivalent word in our language. Think of the sound you make when you say "walk" but drop the
k sound. This was Rick Ban's favorite expression. Rick was a living legend in our formative years. In junior high he was a loner—a large, really
strange-looking kid with a huge head, big ears and little eyes who some
people made fun of.

"Toad [a sad, ugly little orphan girl from the Baptist Home] is fine
and no one's finer,

'cept Rick Ban and Allen Criner."

Pennsylvania with over six hundred kids in our class. They had maybe thirty in the Margaretville High class of 1969 and they seemed more like a big batch of brothers and sisters than anything else. It was there we met the Mountain. Bill Kapitko was a big handsome farm boy from a Russian family up on Hubbell Hill. (You guessed it, Stinky's brother.) I don't know where he got the name Mountain but it suited him. I have never met anyone who could be so cocky, generous, thoughtful, fun loving, dangerous and hilarious all at once. He just gave off a tangible aura of "goddamn! This is fun, aint it?" no matter what the occasion.

Mountain sized us up after the ceremony he had starred in and evidently decided we had some potential.

"So you boys are at Roland's huh? How are the cows treatin' you? Tell you what. Come to our party—let's see how these country beers taste. What do you say?"

The other star we met at the graduation was Clarke Sanford. He was shorter than Mountain, with black hair, shining eyes, and a smile that can only be called "mischievous." Clarke first got our attention when, much to everyone's delight, he leapt across the stage to get his diploma and swept the woman who was handing them out right off

---

That sort of thing. Ban never seemed to care and by sophomore year our friends had realized that he was a genius in many ways—especially in his ability to mold the English language for his own special purposes.

"Waugh!" he would explain loudly when something amused or delighted him. Another good Banism was this important truth only he had discovered: "Hajah spelled backwards is still Hajah." When asked once about how a promising date in a downstairs 'rec' room had gone, he simply said: "Waugh. Things were going great until they ran her parents in on us."

her feet with a huge bear hug and a kiss. The place went up for grabs. Faye told us it was his mother when she stopped laughing and clapping. When John V.B. introduced us to Clarke after the ceremony the first thing he said through an enormous smile was, "Let's go have a taste!"

Well, the party was, as Lee Marvin said in Cat Balloo, "just......swell."

Since we had crawled out of our car in the back yard of the farm on our birthday, we had been either working, eating, talking to Roland, Faye or Gram, sleeping and/or dreaming of working while sleeping. Suddenly we were standing in a raucous room surrounded by people our own age, some of whom were very pretty girls with beers in their hands. It occurred to me that being a farmhand for a summer might not be a punishment for some forgotten evil childhood act after all; it might just turn out to be, as Gram would later say, "the cat's meow."

Another beauty of Faye and Rolly, probably taken at
someone's party a few years before we worked at the farm.
I am completely baffled by the coat and tie.

chapter five

With all the aggravation that two fairly-clueless and disreputable college boys would provide for the Boss that summer I only saw Roland mad twice. Think about that. Not only was he the nicest man I ever worked for, he could do the most amazing things as if they were so perfectly normal they didn't even merit notice. Take, for instance, the day early in July when John and Guzzy threatened a painters' strike on account of the wasps. Now these two might not show up real early but they were the happiest painters I've ever seen. If you walked by Guzzy while he was up on a ladder he would invariably glance down and say, "Schmeeer-in' it on here, Boss!" in a loud cheerful voice, just to let you know that the work was going well.

But not this morning; the boys were grounded. They were standing against the back of the house near where one of the mysterious unused doors to the living room came out, talking to Rol, and their nerves were shot. I listened in, out of a natural desire to show solidarity with other members of the working class, and they were presenting a good argument about how these giant wasps were making it impossible to schmeeer it. John V.B. was scratching his head and glancing up at the big overhanging fascia with a worried expression on his face looking like a Phrygian priest presenting the Gordian Knot to Alexander the Great for his careful inspection. (It seemed that important.) Rolly was

listening patiently when the biggest wasp I had ever seen
flew up right in his face. He didn't even flinch. When it was
almost in his ear he casually reached up, snatched it out of
the air, squashed it between his thumb and a meaty finger
and flicked it away—all in one smooth magnificent motion.
Never said a word. Just kept standing there as if waiting to
hear the rest of the argument. The three of us were dumb-
founded. Guzzy and John looked at each other for a long
moment until finally John shrugged.

"Well!" he said.

Then Guzzy smiled.

"Well," he added. "Guess we better be getting back to
work then."

And that was that.

With the strike averted the boys would paint every
morning as much as they deemed important while George
and I were out various places manipulating the hay. In the
afternoons, after a brief vesper service with the Gram blanket, it was back to the fields. But now we went out as a team.

It worked like this: the four of us would take a tractor,
hitch up a big flat hay wagon and head off to whatever field
had new bales lying in it. When we got there one guy would
drive the rig slowly between two rows of bales while two
others hustled along to pick them up on either side and
throw them aboard while the fourth would be up on the
wagon bed catching and stacking. When everyone is working in sync it flows well, but none of it was easy. I don't know
what those bales weighed exactly but they seemed pretty
heavy, especially at the beginning of the summer, and you
had to grab them by the two twine strands along the top that
held them together, swing them back by your hip and let
them fly upwards so they land somewhere reasonably close

to the person on the wagon. (God allowed the invention of leather gloves specifically for this job.) Of course, the more hay you have picked up the higher off the ground that target gets.

If you were on the wagon you had to be placing all of those new arrivals in neat well-packed rows, with each level running perpendicular to the one below so the load would kind of lock itself together, and there was no stopping once you got going. One might think the man driving the tractor had a cake walk during all of this but speed as well as aim was crucial and you had to really pay attention—three lives were in your hands if you screwed up.[10]

The feeling we always shared on the ride back to the barn, though, was worth all that sweat and trauma. There is nothing like sitting up on top of a full hay wagon on a beautiful summer day with those giant Catskill Cumuli Nimbus hanging in that big blue sky above you, and taking deep breaths of the hay-scented country air. Nothing like it unless the damned Allis Chalmers suddenly decides to pop

---

10. I thought Roland's bales were heavy until one day he took George and me down the valley to help these two gigantic neighbors, Lloyd and Teleford Butler, with one of their fields. These guys were like Catskill cartoon characters. They were huge, I mean fairy tale big and they talked to each other in what was apparently a private family language because we couldn't understand anything they said. It would have been really funny except these crazy fuckers set their baler up to create Butler Brother Bales. I swear the first one I picked up weighed 75 pounds or more and I thought it had to be a mistake; it wasn't. They all did. That was a shitty afternoon. I asked Faye later where somebody gets a name like Teleford and also what they might have been saying to each other. She told me two important things: 1) Teleford had been named after the doctor who delivered him and: 2) "what you thought was a foreign language, John, was just those boys speaking 'New Kingston.'"

out of gear on you which it did one day, on only the second field we had hayed together, coming down off of one of the farm's steepest hills.

Jesus Christ on a Crutch. I was driving and the other guys started shouting and I was terrified and the only thing for it was to aim the whole careening mess at the tiny little bridge of grass and dirt that spanned the deep ditch at the bottom of that field. All four of us were yelling at the top of our lungs when we hit that gap and sailed into the next field and then (blessed saints) finally began to level off and slow down. I'll never forget the smiles on John and Guzzy and George's faces when I turned around after we stopped and I had wrestled the son of a bitch back into gear.

"How'd you like that boys?" I asked, doing the best Roland impression I could come up with under the circumstances. After that day we really were a team I think. Nothing like the fear of certain death to build a little trust into a relationship.

Now, if you could just cruise slowly back to the barn and turn over your load to someone else this haying business wouldn't have seemed so hard. Fun even. But if driving a full wagon up the steep ramp and through what seemed like an impossibly tiny opening into the upstairs part of the barn where the hay was stored wasn't frightening enough, what came next was. The top of the barn was a simple corridor from one end to the other. On either side were cavernous empty holes, called mows, two stories deep. All those bales you had so carefully stacked on that wagon had to be tossed down into the mow of choice and carefully stacked again. If it was your turn to be one of the guys up on the wagon it was one thing but for the two down below, especially on a hot day, it could be like stopping off to visit your dead great uncle (the one who had been such a prick to everybody), at his new home in Dante's Third Circle of Hell.

Especially if one of the throwers, not mentioning any names...but, say your brother, felt that your naked back one day was too tempting a target to pass on and decided to land a bale or three on you for fun. The Hindu Baptist in me worries that it may take several lifetimes to forgive and forget that.

Part of the old barn taken from the circular driveway.
I am reminded of this old saying found later in a book about the
Progressive Era called *Rendezvous With Destiny*:
'God created the wheelbarrow in order to teach the Irish
how to walk on their hind legs.' That's awful cold,
but I wish now that I could have shared it with Rufus.
Pretty sure he would have loved it.

chapter six

Here is something that may not have impressed you as yet, gentle reader. After all of that—the early dawn wake up, morning milking, breakfast, preparing the fields, lunch, and an afternoon spent throwing bales—it was time to milk again. Weeping Blue-Eyed Jesus.[11] Thomas Jefferson once called farmers "the chosen people of God." Thanks a lot, God. Back to the barn to do it all over again to forty some cows. Before dinner.

I'm an olde farte now, (rugby spellings) and yes, I did all of this that summer, but sometimes I look back and find it hard to believe anybody could work so many hours every day. The most amazing thing is, after that first week or so—what the early Jamestown settlers (dying like bewildered chickens under Queen Malaria's axe) called "the seasoning time"—it was easy. Not only was it easy, but it seemed perfectly normal. And, after hooking up with Guz and John V.B. and Clarke and Mountain, it also seemed perfectly normal that any given twelve or thirteen-hour day was just a prelude to the fun you were going to have that night.

At the heart of the mystery was a bar in Margaretville called Lange's. It took us a few weeks to get used to the idea that we could walk in there and order a Genesee Beer, (or

---

11. Jeffery Hunter in *The King of Kings*. Also see: Max Von Sydow in *The Greatest Story Ever Told*. It makes one wonder if the people responsible for casting these movies ever met anyone who was actually from the Middle East.

a Shafer's or a Utica Club), and either Bob Lange or his wife Ann would happily fill a couple of frosty ones up from the tap. In Pittsburgh they didn't even sell beer in the supermarkets, much less in the gas stations; you had to be twenty-one and go to a "beer distributor." These were dank, sacred places which often were only giant garages behind someone's run-down house up against a cliff in godforsaken towns with names like Carnegie or Langley. Minimum purchase: a case. It was a seriously adult business carried on by big men in dirty wife beater T-shirts whose armpits smelled like onion pizza. But here in New York State any eighteen-year-old child could stroll into a tavern and order a draught and a shot of 151 rum back and nobody seemed to care.

What is it about Beer? Other than one or two tentative experiments George and I had avoided contact with the elusive malted beverage until winter of senior year in high school. At that point we began to hang out some week-end nights with a few trusted friends at the "Beer God," an ancient stone barbecue pit safely up the hill from the parking lot in Mount Lebanon Park. Standing there in the cold and dark sharing our secret stash we began to see the world in a different, more dangerous and certainly funnier light. But where, you might ask, did the beer come from? {Is the statute of limitations up yet?} It came from an ingenious procurement method known simply as "garaging."

Let's face it, this was criminal behavior rationalized as necessary and disguised as fun. A team of three or four would cruise through a neighborhood—never our own of course—looking for caches in various open garages. Remember in this strange city you had to buy brewskies by the case, so people did this and then often stored them in stacks in their garages. As the car crawled down the street at maybe fifteen miles an hour on a soft summer evening, alert scouts would call out potential targets.

"Three cases Iron City; two-thirty-four; right side near the back."

"Possible five, make that seven cases Black Label, uh, number 307, left side just inside the door."

And someone would carefully record this information in a small notebook. Coming back after dark, it was really important to get these details right as you didn't want to drop into someone's garage only to find shovels and rakes and power tools (which have a habit of falling over when you can't see them and making a lot of unwanted noise) where you thought there was beer. If that were to happen you might get a dog or even a human being charging out of nowhere. The easiest way to do it was the most direct approach where you simply pull into the driveway (and this was a favorite tactic if the home owner had perchance closed his garage door) with the headlights blazing, throw open the door and grab what you could before retreating. I only saw that done once out of desperation, because this was akin to yelling: "Call the police! We're here!" Much more often a silent commando approach was used: slip in, take some but not all of the treasure, and be gone with no one the wiser.

Personally, my favorite garaging moment occurred one warm night when Rick Ban and I had ventured into a quiet garage on our hands and knees but got stymied somewhere in the middle of it unable to locate our target.

"Jesus, Rick, it's dark in here," I whispered.

"Waugh, no problem," he answered, whipping out a tiny flashlight and flicking it on. For some reason I found that hilarious but wrong—as if we had crossed a distinct border line into professional criminal activity. Well, we gathered up a couple of cases of suddenly-illuminated Blue Ribbon Beer and got about half way down the driveway with them when a loud male voice from our right broke the silence.

"You there! What are you doing? Stop!"

The Dark Menace came running across the lawn and it looked like certain jail time, but just as he got to us he stopped and broke into laughter. It was Bob Bennet, the rhythm guitar player in our rock band, the Quaker Blues. He had come outside on the porch next door while we were inside and was kissing his girlfriend goodnight when he spied some burglars and heroically ran to stop them.

"You guys are beautiful!" he yelled. "Get the hell out of here, are you out of your minds, hitting Linda's neighbors like this?"

And off we sped. Lest you think that we made a career out of this kind of behavior, keep in mind that George and I only went on a few of these expeditions. Uh...maybe several. But what is it about beer that makes young men do such ridiculous things? There's definitely something in the water. And that something played a big role in our Catskill summer. Looking back, maybe the Beer God was watching over his wayward children; who can say?[12]

Anyway, it felt good to finally be legitimate and our new best friend, Bob Lange, was perfect. He had the rough

---

12. For those who fear that our new-found love affair with beer may have taken us beyond common theft into a realm of extended moral degeneracy, I should note that after the snow finally disappeared that spring five or six of us went up to visit the Beer God and picked up the hundreds of empty cans and bottles we had left there. It seems Boy Scouts not only taught us how to swear but also some valuable lessons about effectively policing a campsite.

good looks of Mike Nelson from *Sea Hunt* which is to say he looked like a grizzled trucker with light brownish red hair worn in a tasteful Elvis/greaser style, side burns and all. We loved him deeply. Bob never even carded us—hell, we were old men by the way they reckoned such things in the Catskills. (A local legend had it that Guzzy was once allowed to bartend somewhere at the age of fourteen.) There were several other bars in Margaretville, the Pioneer, Dick's, but "Uncle Bob" had our attention and devotion. Ann seemed surly at first, or maybe it was the gigantic beehive hairdo that put me off. She sensed soon enough, however, that George and I were in a kind of nouveaux-religious state in her place—supplicants at the altar...our first legal bar—and treated us well. She also made the best hot meat ball sandwiches in this quadrant of the galaxy.

Most nights we would connect with one or more of our new friends and just drift into some adventure, but one evening early on George was courting Claire at her parent's home just across the road from the farm and I found myself alone at Bob's. You could hear the most amazing things in there if you could get any of the old boys to talk to you, which proved fairly easy because I was dressed like them and smelled vaguely like a barn. You never really lose that odor when you've been in one four or five hours a day, shower or not. We had let our own reddish-brown hair grow out a bit and both of us sported mustaches that put some of the older people off at first, but when they learned we were farmin' it at Roland's, things were fine.

That night, sitting at the bar, I got into a serious discussion about life in the mountains with an old farmer. The guy was massive, but grizzled and stooped. He told me that the truest thing he ever heard about this place was a warning someone down along the Hudson River had given when asked by a stranger where the Catskill Mountains actually started.

"Go up a ways and when you get to where there's two rock for every dirt, you're there," he said, laughing at the old saying.

"I don't know why anyone would want to farm in a place like that," he added sadly.

When it seemed time to head home I had a choice to make. There were two ways to get to town from the farm, the long way out along the New Kingston Valley road (which had its charms because you could stop at Mary Schebesta's on route 30 and buy road beer out of a big cooler on her porch), or the shorter hop up over the steep Margaretville Mountain road. It can get supernaturally foggy on this road at night and George and I usually only took that one together to counter the fact that on the way back from whatever place we had been partying, you couldn't see anything. I mean it all disappeared. On a night like that, whoever was driving would have to pull to the far-left side of the road—that would be the wrong one—and steer by the branches and leaves barely visible out the side window. We called it the "Lucky Lindy" approach because Charles Lindberg had flown all the way to fucking Paris without being able to see through a front windshield, and it was better than the pilot seeing nothing. This strategy entails some risk which is why it was good to have somebody riding shotgun to stare hard ahead into the gloom to look for oncoming headlights.

That particular night it was clear enough, but I had gotten so absorbed in my talk with the ancient one that driving even on a deserted road was a poor idea at best. Well,

I went up over the hill and made it to Bet and Jerry's where I decided to drop the car off with George, leaving myself just a short walk up to the farm. He and Claire were hanging out in the living room trying to be very quiet so they could kiss and things and not disturb her mother trying to sleep upstairs. Even in my sorry condition I realized I was somewhat unwanted, although I was probably entertaining them well enough until I got up to leave and fell heavily on to the glass coffee table in the middle of the room. Time to go. Out the door and down the hill to the road, leaving them to explain the great crashing noise to Betty without the problem of having to translate anything I might have added to that conversation.

Now it was just a question of navigating the long winding driveway up to Rolly's great farmhouse and bed. Don't ever assume, just because you can say, "I'm walking home" that you are guaranteed making it. Gram said, "there are always complications," and I should have been listening to my inner Gram that night because I almost didn't. I must have been almost as drunk as Dumbo and his little rat friend were when they got into the sauce and had to deal with the psychedelic nightmare of those Pink Elephants on Parade. No hallucinations for me, but I was so toasted I should have had a designated walker. When I got to the little private bridge that crossed the stream running alongside the road on the farm side, it seemed so peaceful and nice there that I sat down half-way across, with my legs dangling over the edge, to listen to the water gurgling happily on its way.

Borrowing a trick from Rip Van Winkle, I evidently decided to take a short nap in the wrong place. Unlike young Rip's poor choice, which only cost him twenty years or so, mine was very nearly the last more-or-less conscious decision of my life. The next thing I knew Wee Wee was shaking me and holding me and pretty much sobbing. She had come barreling up the road and turned into the driveway and just happened to see my white tee shirt stretched out in her headlights before screaming to a stop with her tires inches from my head. She said (the next morning) she didn't know for sure whether to laugh or cry so she did both at the same time because when Wee Wee tried to wake me at first on the bridge I sat up, looked at her in amazement, and said quite clearly: "Keep the goddamned cows away from me."

Whew.

After a night like that, of course, getting up to work at the first sniff of dawn can be a problem, but with one glaring exception we never failed to get down to the barn for milking shortly after Rolly would appear at the bedroom door and say: "Time to go boys."

I realized in early July that I had a friend in the barn who could help me through some of those rocky mornings, but this affection caught the attention of a certain canine with an eye for mischief. The first job in the morning was getting the cows into the barn and into their milking stalls. This was usually remarkably easy, as they would be bunched up just outside the big back doors in a muddy area where the manure track exited the lower barn, waiting patiently for the Boss to open things up from the inside. It was during those few minutes before the grand entrance that I would find one of the largest of the ladies, a delightfully gentle creature named Big Red, nestle my head upon her massive shoulders and get a little more precious sleep. We developed quite a sturdy relationship, but the problem was that Rufus could see I trusted that cow.

Big Red still had her horns, one of only two in the herd claiming that distinction, and she had a special place down towards the milk room. It was in the second row, and you didn't push the normal metal gate-like thing (that kept the cows confined in their stalls) over her head, because it wouldn't fit, but instead hooked her collar to a short chain. She was always nice to me so I got in the habit of bending directly over her head to do this. One morning Rufus waited until that exact moment—that special window of vulnerability—then he came tearing down the back of the row nipping at her heels with a ferocious growl. Terrified, Big Red bellowed and jacked her head straight up in the air. I had a moment of bizarre clarity while flying through space that the dog had set me up and then I slammed into some hay bales stacked against the nearest wall.

That cow pitched me a good six to eight feet and the force of her head, not to mention landing, knocked the wind clear out of me. As I slowly got to my feet trying to decide whether I had been killed I saw Rufus sitting up in his wheelbarrow laughing at me. You don't have to believe this, but a dog can laugh at you. He was immensely proud of his timing, I suppose, and was savoring the moment. It would be easy to say that I learned a valuable lesson that morning, but about two weeks later he got me again. Exactly the same way. Of course, if Big Red had connected with her huge horns either time, I would have been gored meat, but Rufus was evidently willing to take that chance in the interest of a good practical joke.

Other than Ginger, who was a cunt, no other cow in Roland's barn ever exhibited a moment of violent or even skittish behavior towards George and me once they got used to us. Perhaps it was the music. One of the first things the

Boss would do to prepare for milking was to turn on an old beat up transistor radio that sat up on the ledge of a small window nobody had been able to see anything through for a hundred years. Same station, early morning or late afternoon, and it played nothing but muzak. The kind of banal horror you only heard back then when pushing a grocery cart through the A&P or riding in an elevator. I have often wondered what planet that station came from, Uranus maybe, because it was physically painful to listen to. Probably the second or third morning in the barn I worked up the courage to ask Roland to change the channel but he only smiled and said: "Nope. The cows love this stuff. It keeps them happy."

That program manager is floating in Purgatory just now, but he did something as the summer progressed that guarantees he will be released eventually. He chose two songs off the AM charts and played them often, and I smile even today when I hear them because they may have saved our sanity. At least once during every turn in the barn *Crystal Blue Persuasion* by Tommy James and the Shondells and *Love Can Make You Happy* (by some one-hit wonders) came on that goddamned radio. These are not the greatest songs of the summer of `69 by any means, but for me it was like that magic moment when Jesus ignores the burly Roman guard and offers Charlton Heston a life-saving drink of water during the "Burning Desert" scene in *Ben Hur*. Never has so little meant so much to so few.

To combat that long ugly daily dose of the worst music ever recorded, whoever got up to milk would come back to the bedroom and wake the other one up for breakfast by putting on a recording of Tom Rush quietly singing Joni Mitchell's *Urge for Going*, or *The Shadow Dream Song*. And that, even more so than the wonderful tunes on the radio and juke boxes every night from bands like Creedence, Janis, and the Who, became the sound track for life on the farm. Strange that a sad song about the end of summer should have been the way we started many mornings, but it's just so damned beautiful it seemed perfect.

> I woke up today and found
> The frost perched on the town.
> It hovered in a frozen sky, and gobbled summer down.
> When the sun turns traitor cold
> And shivering trees are standing in a naked road,
> I get the urge for going, but I never seem to go.

The second verse starts out a little more encouraging: "I had a girl in summer time with summer colored skin. And not another man in town, my darlin's heart could win." I had a girl in summer time. Well, not quite. I had one date early that summer and it was a disaster. More like the Andrea Doria going down off Nantucket than the Titanic in mid-ocean, because the casualties weren't as steep, but it's a painful memory anyway. Her name was Liz and I met her at that first high school party—even kissed her briefly. She was a Stamford girl, a town about twenty-five miles north-west of Margaretville. She had seemed cheerful and pretty and interested then, and so one night I drove all the way out there to see her. It had great potential: a case of Shafer beer and a T.V. set in a den and an empty house and you can only imagine the thoughts swirling through my nineteen-year-old brain. Sad stories should be brief; I'll only say it became apparent early on that she was more interested in drinking the beer than kissing me. A lot more interested. Pleading the

eleventh amendment—the one about having to get up early—
I drove quietly back to the farm feeling pretty low. Turned
out to be a very good thing, I suppose. If that night had gone
differently the summer might have been filled with "complications" perhaps neither of us needed.

George, meanwhile, was living on the edge of heaven
because Becky Hartman finally did arrive at the Van Benschoten's door one perfect afternoon. She was even more
perfect than I remembered. For all of Gram's uncharacteristi-
cally petulant behavior upon first hearing the news, she was
nice enough to the new guest. You couldn't help but love
Becky even if you were a pissed off eighty-year-old woman...
that's how perfect she was. But Becky Hartman brought two
great sorrows into my life that summer. The first was obvious: she was there to romance George. Although I never
had the courage to ask him about it, I don't think anything
happened beyond some interesting kissing for old time's
sake.[13] Christ, I hope not; I'm still jealous. The unexpected
part was far worse. The day she left she deposited a female
time of month souvenir in the bathroom toilet upstairs and
it jammed up the whole septic system.

No one growing up in a city could have known any better—I certainly didn't. But Roland did and he took it hard.
He didn't get mad, he just took us out to the back yard that
morning, handed us two shovels and said:

"I don't know exactly where the tank is boys, it's been so
long, but start digging and by and by you'll find it."

---

13. Sorry. I know that if this ever gets turned into a screen play, that
kind of limited disclosure will make many people in L.A. disgusted, but I
warned you. It's not that kind of Tall Tale.

This is George, taken by Claire that summer.
Handsome devil....no wonder Becky liked him better.

George took all this fairly well for someone whose romantic interlude had just literally turned to shit, but I can't say that I was that brave. For me it was a close race between grief and anger right then and every shovel thrust that hit a rock (two for every dirt) made it worse. That was a long morning and afternoon—the haying had to wait for that giant hole to get dug. But on the brighter, educational side of things two suburban boys who had never even heard of a septic tank before eventually got to see one up close.

There were other days when we didn't hay it. I mentioned that it only rained at night that Camelot summer, but sometimes when it did, depending on how long and how much, you had to let things dry out. Roland was as much a genius at weather as he was in directing the haying operation. He spent a lot of time considering wind direction and strength and could tell from this and the cloud patterns what was coming and when. After a lifetime in that valley he could put a satellite to shame. There was only one mistake that I noticed, but it led to one of the worst jobs. Deep in his haying fever one day he had George rake a field into rows and he didn't get around to baling it and they all got soaked that night. He wasn't in a mood to discuss things the next morning, but re-raking by tractor wouldn't work for some reason so the long hay rows had to be turned over to dry by hand. By pitchfork, actually, and that was another long ugly tedious morning. At first our Ivy League educations came in handy and we pretended to be medieval serfs at work in the fields of the Lord. But that game only worked for the first fifteen minutes so I can't really recommend the experience of doing things on a farm the "old fashioned" way.

Our Once and Future Catskill Mountain Companions. It was taken, evidently, during a visit to Cape Cod that summer which the twins could not participate in due to work related issues. John V.B. and Clarke are in the second (top of car) row, left to right. Guzzy is 2nd from the left in the (hood) row, and Mountain, naturally, is the one sporting the perfect hat. I have no idea who the other guys are, much less the pretty girls. They never came to visit us in New Kingston.

chapter seven

One day, and the timing on this was unbelievable, rainy weather created a window where the Boss didn't have anything pressing and it allowed us to take the first great road trip of the summer. Clarke had suffered an unwelcome guest for more than a week. Some rich kid he met at Cape Cod—the Sanford's had a bit of money floating around in the family—took him up on one of those offers nobody is supposed to take you up on and came to visit him in the mountains. We hadn't seen much of Clarke for a week or so, but that was not unusual. Any given night one or more of the boys might be off with a girlfriend. John V.B. and Clarke both had steady ones, Madeline and Melinda, beautiful names, beautiful girls...ooowheee. Even Guz had a 'squeeze,' as we sometimes said back then. Her name was Sharon, and she was very pale, with long black hair. Guzzy called her "The Ghost" and it fit; she was rarely around and when she was she didn't seem to be part of whatever we were doing, remaining a quiet enigma. Our friends had other distractions as well so we never knew when the long work day ended who we would see or even how the program would read. Those nights just came at us one at a time with a beautiful rhythm and it seemed there was always some unforeseen adventure beckoning.

Anyway, Clarke was saddled with this screwball named Drew who was evidently the kind of person who woke up every morning genetically incapable of making a single good choice for the rest of the day. When he met you, for example, he would hold out his hand and say:

"My name is Drew; how do you do?"

This was so goofy it had the potential to be charming, but the guy was such a fuck up it didn't work that way. Roswell Sanford, Clarke's father and, incidentally, owner/editor of *The Catskill Mountain News*, wanted to kill the kid already, but when Drew took his son's beautiful sports car out for an unauthorized spin with a girl and put it into a tree, it was time for him to go. Of course, he had no money with him—I don't even know how he got there—so there was nothing for it but to drive Drew back to Boston to get rid of him. Mountain didn't think it would be safe for Clarke to go alone with this cartoon character and since the cow hands and the painters suddenly happened to be free for a day because of the rain, we all signed on for a dash to New England. Unfortunately for our new brotherhood, John's mother wouldn't let him go. Was it Jerry's doing, or was she just exhibiting some casual motherly common sense?

When Clarke showed up at the farm that morning in his grandmother's Jeep Wagoneer he jumped out and looked George and I over carefully.

"My dad's pretty mad at you two, you know," he said with a grin. "He's taken a lot of grief over that thing you sent to the paper, so I thought I had better come pick you up here."

That was certainly understandable; nobody wants to be remembered as the guy who printed a letter from a dog. But the Sanford's big SUV before they had SUV's was perfect for a road trip. It had room for all of us and came equipped with cases of beer courtesy of the outstanding credit the family name conjured up in Margaretville. Clarke also happened to have one of the greatest laughs on this planet—somewhere between a maniacal cackle and a snort—and he liked to drive a lot and he liked to drive fast, which left the rest of us free to enjoy the scenery and the cold concoctions and engage in some mild Drew baiting.

We collected that sorry specimen at the Margaretville Hospital and took him to a quick goodbye hearing at the Justice of the Peace. This may be hard to fathom, but court was being held above Solly Darling's Laundromat in Fleischmans, a nearby town. It's normal in these mountains to elect a person who has a good head on their shoulders to be the local judge; doesn't matter what they might do for a living as long as they are intelligent and trustworthy. Capital idea, but imagine our consternation at the time—we are escorting the guilty party to a fucking laundromat?

Anyway, teasing Drew on that trip never lasted long. He was wearing a white bandanna-like bandage around his head, a souvenir from when he bounced the expensive car off the tree, and he was just so pathetic that we understood our true mission was just to get him out of the Catskills, not to torture anyone any further. Besides, anytime he started to talk too much, Clarke would smile over at him and say, "shut up Drew," and this seemed to work pretty well.

I can't remember if the original plan was to go all the way to the Cape or not, but by the time we got into one of the little rundown suburbs of Boston—Medfahd, Bedfahd, Dedham?—our boy behind the wheel had had enough. In a farewell scene worthy of Hollywood, he pulled the Wagoneer over to the curb by a grocery store, pulled out some cash and told Drew to go in and buy a six pack of Narragansett tall boys. When he came back to the passenger side window with the beer, Clarke leaned over Guzzy and said:

"Great. Thanks. Here, you take one and hand over the rest."

Drew did just that.

"Thanks again. See ya. It's been unbelievable," Clarke said and drove off, leaving his houseguest with a quizzical goof ball smile on his face. I remember being able to see that white bandage for several blocks before it faded into the urban landscape.

"Thank God. Where's Harvard?" Clark shouted. "I want to see how the other half lives!"

The next thing you know we're piling out of the Jeep in front of Stoughton Hall in the Harvard Yard on a perfect summer early afternoon and George is pointing out the fourth floor windows to his freshman-year dorm room.

"Alright, this was home last year. My room was up there. The window on the left is the one my brother here made the mistake of sticking his head out of late one night to yell at Sorenson, that crazy fuck from Utah."

Rich Sorenson had been George's other grad school proctor who lived on the first floor with Andy Van Benschoten. Rich was really wasted that night and was making a fuss of some sort out in front of the hall, so I thought it would be fun to harass him a little. But he was in no mood to be yelled at by any stupid freshman, especially a visiting one.

"He was standing about where you are Guz, when he let that tennis ball fly," George was remembering fondly. "Greatest throw I ever saw."

I had been forced to admit the sheer athletic brilliance of it later, a few days after the vision returned in my right eye.

Cambridge was certainly beautiful that day, but the 'urge for going' must have been on Clarke's mind 'wicked haad' as they say there, because pretty soon he jumped up from the grass where we were lounging and smiled that wicked smile.

"Hey!" he asked. "Have you two guys ever been to New York City?"

"Not since we were little kids," I said.

"Well what do you think, Mountain, shall we show them 42nd Street?"

And we were off.

On the way down the boys started reminiscing about their Senior Trip, earlier that spring. In tiny rural New York high schools the classes are so small that they are able to go on a two or three day bus trip together near the end of senior year. Naturally, the teacher who is the class adviser and the other chaperones need to be on guard against the smuggling of alcohol and other contraband so that the school board and parents can safely assume things are under control when their little darlings are traveling to far away strange places.

Well these seniors had a plan, which Mountain explained to us on our way south.

"We wanted to do something special no one had ever pulled off before—something really memorable—so we had an Alamo Party."

On a pre-arranged signal, they had ditched the adult supervision and the rest of the class, rendezvoused at a cheap hotel and rented a room. The rest was both simple and heroic: they made a stand.

"Everybody pooled their money; we bought as much beer as we could carry and went into the room and barricaded the door to the outside world with the stacked cases. Then we drank our way out."

Mountain's eyes almost teared up as he told us this, he was still that proud of how well the tiny garrison had performed against overwhelming odds.[14]

The Wagoneer pulled into Manhattan just as the sun was setting. I remember the glow of the orange light reflecting on the windows of the impossibly tall buildings that surrounded us. I also remember feeling very much like a farm boy getting his first view of the big city. Clarke happened to notice the looks of awe on George's and my face as we craned our necks to look up at the skyscrapers.

"Better close your mouths, you two," he said. "That's a dead giveaway to these people. If they sense you're from out of town they'll rip you to shreds."

He maneuvered us into the lower East Village. We were on a mission to find a legendary bar the boys had heard about called McSorley's. Mountain described the rumors.

"They say when you order a draft, the bartender hands you two glasses of beer. Each. No explanation. It's a tradition going back to the mid 1800's. Also, no women are allowed in the place, period."

----

14. The senior trip is really quite a sacred legacy in the Catskills and an earlier one played an enormous role in our story. Roland had pneumonia and missed going with his class but it was so important a rite of passage that he went the next year with the class behind him. And it so happened that a young woman named Faye Liddle was also along because her school, Andes, was too small to mount a trip of its own. Somewhere on the bus ride to the Delaware Water Gap, Roland asked if he could sit next to her, and the rest is, shall we say, history?

Faye told me years later that Rol bought her a drink at the top of the Empire State Building that made her "very dizzy." "The trip was not well-chaperoned," she added.

I didn't think much of that part of the tradition, having just spent a remarkably girl-less year at an all men's school in the Berkshire Mountains, but the historical aspect was intriguing, and McSorley's did not disappoint in the least. When we found it and walked in, the place was empty of people but it seemed enormously cluttered. Every square inch of the wall space was covered with pictures and memorabilia from the past, and the floor was sprinkled with good old-fashioned saw dust. It was a time travel moment, especially when the surly Irish barkeep did indeed hand us each two glasses of house ale. We gratefully took these to a table in the back of the small tavern where we could soak in the atmosphere without seeming too much like tourists. One customer wandered in but otherwise we were alone back there except for two of the biggest and meanest looking cats I have ever seen, perched on a ledge above the old wainscoting. George went to pet one of them but stopped his hand in mid-air when the big boy looked up and gave him a scowl that said unmistakably: 'don't even fucking think about touching me.' Guzzy was impressed.

"Yep, better leave those fat bastards alone," he said. "They could kill all of us."

Next stop was 42nd street.

"You won't believe this place," Clarke said. "Wall to wall hookers and pimps!"

Forty-second street was a let-down after McSorley's. I guess I had seen crappy parts of cities before between Pittsburgh and Detroit and I was developing a strong desire to get the hell out of a place where so many people were jammed together ugly and back to the solitude of the New Kingston Valley. Clarke insisted we have at least one beer and picked the rattiest toilet he could find where we lined up along the bar for a farewell-to-the-city toast. While the bartender was occupied in the back room, Sanford reached over and quietly unscrewed the handle to the tap we had ordered beers from.

"Souvenir," he said with a big smile as he slipped it in his pocket, and we were soon heading back to the mountains and the ever-waiting cows.

Roland seemed to know that young men needed room to act crazy and stupid from time to time and left us free to make whatever mistakes we had coming. As I mentioned, I only saw him angry twice and only once directly at me and I certainly deserved it for the unruly behavior John V.B. and I exhibited the magic night that Budweiser went off strike. He didn't even get angry over the stunt George pulled on another occasion. In a classic case of 'you only want what you can't have,' we had all developed a mighty yearning for the King of Beers simply because we couldn't have any. A strike by somebody somewhere along the flow chart had caused Bud to disappear from the Catskills that summer and so we were open to any suggestion in our ongoing quest to find some.

One night when the haying crew was loose on the world Guz allowed that there was a place we hadn't tried yet where only old tourists and Brothers from the city went— an ancient hotel called The Friendship Manor. I think now that he hadn't thought of it before because The Friendship Manor was like something James Hilton had in mind when he wrote *Lost Horizon*; there was some kind of protective energy shield around it that only let you visit once in a great while. Maybe only once. Hell, I'm not even sure the place was real. It was hard to find and we drove places I could never reconstruct to get there and then there was this massive old grand stair case before us leading up to the entrance of a hotel that looked a hundred and fifty years old and seemed to be glowing with a mysterious potential.

If the elusive beverage was to be found anywhere in these mountains this had to be it and sure enough the kindly old black bartender set out ice cold long neck bottles of the King as if he had been waiting for us all summer. It was dark in there and huge—the bar itself was long and massive, hand carved oak no doubt—and I remember thinking that I was somehow home...really home and safe and then it all went suddenly south in a great rush. We had just been served a second round, no less glorious than the first one, and I was saying something to Guzzy on my left when we heard this ungodly cracking sound that could only safely be described as wood meeting human skull and I whirled right to find an empty bar stool where only a moment before George had been sitting.

He was gone. Well, not exactly. He was on the floor out cold with blood beginning to pool under his head where he had hit the edge of the bar on his way down. The crazy bastard had evidently picked that moment of great serenity and peace to fall asleep. I know there are people who specialize in that sort of thing but George isn't one of them. Looking back, I now understand that the dark magic of this hidden Shangri-La had cast a spell over him causing the Fall from Grace, but at that moment we only knew we had to get out of there immediately. So Guz and I hoisted our fallen comrade to his feet and hauled him between us out the front door onto the porch. It was at this exact moment that George did the one thing certain to guarantee we could never return. He woke up, said, "look out now" and proceeded to hurl all that precious Budweiser and burned ass of cow from dinner out over those beautiful front steps.

Roland actually took it well. I had called him from the emergency room of the Margaretville Hospital (yes...as I mentioned before, there was, thank God, a small one there) to get permission for the doctor to stitch up George's head and he gave it cheerfully. He must have been expecting a call like that for a while.

"Bring him home in one piece if they let you out of there," he said over the phone.

They did want us out of there or at least partitioned away from other emergency room guests, because the night nurse allowed John and Guz and I to wait on the floor of this little storage room filled with hospital supplies. J.V.B. had discovered it in his endless curiosity for new and exciting corners of the world and the nurses must have decided we would be alright in there, at least temporarily. It was a good fit for us because Guzzy had wisely smuggled in some cold Gennys and a pack of cards knowing hospitals have a lot of 'wait' in them. The lack of poker chips was only a minor problem as the shelves provided an array of different bandages and other medical knickknacks that substituted nicely for nickels, dimes and quarters and we soon had a lively game of five card draw going. Nursey was pretty mad at us later when she came in to say we could take our wounded away, but I also think she understood it could have gone much worse, all things considered.

That night the Boss stayed up to tuck us in and make sure George was alright and took it all in stride when we got back to the farm. A week or so later, however—the morning after the Budweiser strike ended —-he hit his limit.

It started innocently enough. I don't remember why no one else was involved in this particular escapade—perhaps because John V.B. knew in his heart it would work better as a small unit commando operation—but he and I started out that night to take care of a situation that had been bothering him all summer. As you come down off the mountain road from Margaretville into the valley you merge into the New Kingston road from the right. It looks like this:

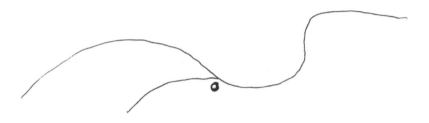

The little circle represents a stop sign. The trouble was that stop sign had been a yield sign as long as anyone could remember. The state police ("Cowboys," as Rolly once called them disgustedly from a field as they flew by) had decided in their wisdom to make people come to a complete stop there even though anyone with a brain cell still functioning could clearly see over their left shoulder far enough down the road to safely yield to anyone coming from Margaretville or Andes that way. Most of the boys cheerfully ignored the new sign, but John took it hard. He explained to me that it was his "by God constitutional right" as an intelligent citizen to make that call and that stop sign was a direct and intentional insult and had to go.

So it went. Several times. John had simply stopped during a couple of late night trips and yanked it out of the ground. The police kept putting it back up as police will, but this last time they had decided on a more permanent structure and cemented the thing in there and she wasn't going to budge. J.V.B. had been stewing on that move for a week or two when he lit upon a brilliant solution.

"We'll paint the bastard red! We'll make it invisible," he declared when he stopped by the farm to pick me up that night in his Mustang. Other than Clarke's sports car, which was still in the hospital from Drew's little joyride, John had the hottest car of any of us: a 1965 green Mustang with a manual shift on the floor and no doubt some serious horse-power lurking under the hood. Normally this vast potential for trouble was not a problem, John being the calmest and quietest of us all, but tonight was different. Tonight he had a crusader look in his eyes—an 'it's time to take Jerusalem back from the Moors' kind of smile, and I was more than happy to be his squire-at-arms.

So we painted it red. But not an ordinary red. It was a deep, rich stop-sign red that John had found on a prepara-tory trip to a paint store in Delhi. He had evidently been waiting anxiously all through haying that day keeping the plan to himself until the last minute when he came to get me so there could be no leaks; no mistakes. First, however, we had to be patient a little longer and wait for the cover of darkness, which is why we drove down to Mary's porch to stock up on some provisions for the raid. Do you remember Christmas morning when you were seven? The first sight of the red stockings and the toys under the tree? That's what Mary's stand up cooler with the sliding door looked like that evening. The two of us stood stunned, gaping at row after row of gaily bedecked red and white and black cans and big brown bottles bearing the long-lost logo of the King.

"Truly, it is a sign from God," John said quietly.

"I think quarts might be the way to go here," I replied, bringing my joy to bear on the logistics of our impending assault on government property. "It gives us the option of keeping our stores secure with the screw-on caps when we 'go in'."

"Good idea," he said.

A quart or so later when it finally got dark enough to go to work, J.V.B. insisted that we had to make our approach from above, and come in dark and hot. That meant coming down the Margaretville Mountain road fast with the headlights off. It was the first of a series of really bad decisions about his Mustang and our driving we were to make that evening. Some summer nights in the Catskills headlights are pretty much irrelevant, but those nights involve a full moon so bright the road is illuminated for hundreds of yards. This one didn't have that kind of moon, but we got close to the bottom of the hill intact anyway. As we had carefully rehearsed during the course of several briefings, as soon as the car came to a halt about twenty-five yards up the hill (half into the ditch on the right) we leaped out and charged the objective. It was a flawless plan. I carried the small can of paint and a screw driver; John led the way with the brush. Everything depended on speed, of course, but we also did not want to leave any clues for the Cowboys and their minions. There was to be no paint spillage, no footprints, no wallets left at the scene to allow them to trace us back to Roland's or Jerry's.

And it went off without casualties. I held the paint and John's brush work was hurried but splendid—every one said so later—even in the bright sunlight it had the look of a professional's touch. We left a perfect stop sign: perfectly smooth and perfectly red, but with the hated order erased, gone, vanished. It was as if some supernatural being reached down overnight and said: "POOF! Look at the amazing thing I have made come to pass."

JVB gunned that car down the road towards New Kingston, lights on now, with the two of us laughing as hard as Brer Rabbit coming out on the fun side of the briar patch. As he went through the gears heading out of the village towards Bovina (we had decided to head deeper into the mountains to elude any chance of hot pursuit) he turned to me.

"You know, the coolest thing about this car is that if you listen carefully you can shift gears without using the clutch." I had never imagined such a thing, but he could do it and so I had to give it a try. The fact that I had left my glasses back at the farm (I only wore them to drive) didn't seem to matter. We were driving by touch, sound and vibration anyway now and we were driving with the new-born King. As horrible and thoughtless as that may seem to you, gentle reader, consider only this: it was extremely rare for anyone else to be on that road after the cows were put out of the barns for the night. Why we were spared, in our madness, from smashing into the assorted deer or porcupine or bear is something you will have to take up with God.

It was late when we got back to the farm but I remember taking at least three or four exciting victory laps around the house before we landed. John and I congratulated each other on a night of groundbreaking success all around and I stumbled out of the car and up to bed. It had been a night of wonder: of portents and signs. And somewhere in our travels we had acquired one that said, "DO NOT PASS." I managed to drag this new acquisition through the dark house and up the stairs and carefully set it up outside the door to our bedroom before turning in.

The next morning was my turn to milk and I slept right through the wake-up call and Faye had to handle all the work of my shift as well as her normal chores and Roland was understandably furious. He didn't yell at me at breakfast or ever raise his voice, yet I felt all day as if I had betrayed a great trust and that things could never again be the same between us. When we got the girls into the barn for the evening milking, however, he turned to George with that twinkle in his eyes and said, "Well...when you boys put up a sign, I believe you mean it." And that was that.

chapter eight

The only other thing I wore my glasses for that summer besides driving (when I was not temporarily insane) was to go to the movies; I never put them on to work. It wasn't just a question of nineteen-year-old vanity. The last place in the world you would need or want glasses is in a dairy barn. Any cow worth a damn would soon see them as a potential target. You might ask: how could such an animal go after one's glasses short of kicking them off your face, or pulling a Big Red? If you have ever spent any time crouching near the business end of a cow trying to attach the suction doohickeys to her teats you know how cruel a weapon her tail can be. Now, cows need their tails to maintain their sanity, living, as they do for a good part of the year as the center of attention for millions of flies; but any farmer ever born (or hired) would love to pay veterinarians like the good Dr. John a small fee to cut them off at birth. The vet might enjoy the job as well, even throw it in for free. The tail of a cow has a mighty reach, and God designed it so that it grows in a place where it can't help but capture and hold little pieces of cow dung.[15] When dried and carefully arranged

---

15. Our bovine friends will, strangely enough, lift their tails high up into the air away from their bodies and lean rigidly forward while performing excretory functions. This is a pretty funny thing to see if you are not used to it. But given the extraordinary quantity of material being processed here it is no wonder the tails retain some choice bits. A related note: unlike dogs, who seem genuinely embarrassed when they realize you are watching them take a dump (and will often give you an endearing look that is very close to a shy smile), cows don't make that big of a deal out of it. "Any time, any place—look out for me" is their motto.

they take on much the same potential for damage as the
little lead pellets woven into a cat-o-nine-tails: the instru-
ment of punishment/torture once employed so effectively
by certain stalwarts of His Majesty's Royal Navy. And that
may be where some twisted ex-farm boy got the idea for
it. Look at the name. Think a cat's tail ever hurt anybody?
Godamned cows. There is nothing quite like getting caught
square across the face by a whipping cow tail soaked in shit.
Experience eventually teaches one to be on guard for it, but
as we have seen, suburban youths can be amazingly ignorant and forgetful on a farm.

But I digress.[16] We only went to two movies that
summer. The first time was when my brother noticed
that *Night of the Living Dead* was showing at the drive-in
in Oneonta, a small city about an hour away. Long before it
reached cult/classic status this movie opened as a cheaply
made B-/C+ horror film in the kind of theaters that would
take the word 'seedy' as a compliment. George had already
seen it with Bob Rosenberg and Roger Weis when the three
new Stoughton Hall entry mates were getting to know each
other by exploring the hidden corners of Boston's 'urban
sub-cultures.' They were wandering about one innocent afternoon in the Combat Zone (a place where sailors on shore
leave gathered to find romance), when they jumped sponta-
neously into a run-down movie house to catch a matinee dou-
ble feature. George remembered our senior year advanced

---

16. If you find such things annoying, don't read *Tristram Shandy*, an
early English novel on my major's reading list at Williams, which is one
gigantic string of bewildering and delightful digressions. Of course,
further distracting a reader by discussing this topic in a footnote would
probably be considered a criminal act in itself by most literary critics.
I guess I'll have to take my chances. Blame Laurence Sterne.

English teacher, Jackie Hughes, mentioning in her pompous way that her father had been an extra in a "wretched thing" called Night of the Living something, filmed outside of Pittsburgh, and warned us never to debase ourselves by watching it. An irresistible review. After enjoying Richard Jaeckel's stunning performance in *The Green Slime*, the freshmen were delighted by the zombie movie—especially George, who realized from the first scene that there is something so relentlessly low-rent-Western-Pennsylvania about the whole thing that it made him homesick.

We took Wee Wee with us to the drive-in and I remember her being dismayed that we couldn't stop laughing at what must have seemed to her an exercise in tasteless grossout. Anyone who grew up in Pittsburgh in the Sixties would forgive us. The dialogue is hilarious enough, but when the director had "Chilly Billy" Bill Cardille (a local hero who was the announcer for both "Studio Wrestling" and "Chiller Theatre" every Saturday night on WIIC Channel 11), play a legitimate news broadcaster, all bets were off. It was a wonderful night.

The only other movie we saw that summer was an even weirder experience. There is a small town near Margaretville called Fleischmans, once a thriving Mecca—that can't be right—of luxury vacation hotels for many of New York City's Jewish communities. It had been a major stop on the vaudeville Borsch Belt, where the Marx Brothers and many others had cut their show business teeth in the Twenties. By 1969, however, it was a seeming ghost town sporting about ten burned-out hotels and one sad little movie theatre. George and I went to a Sunday matinee there to see *Where Eagles Dare* because Richard Burton and Clint 'Rowdy Yates' Eastwood were in it. A fine WWII action yarn, especially if you enjoy watching German soldiers take fatties. What became increasingly strange was just how much this particular full-house audience was enjoying it. They started applauding at the very first sight of Nazi blood, and as the intrepid commandos begin killing Germans by the batch, people began yelling and clapping as if they were at a...well...studio wrestling match in Pittsburgh on a Saturday night watching Bruno Sammartino throw The Sheik around the ring with Bill Cardille urging them on. By the end when the whole mountain blows up—German castle and all—they were on their feet screaming. We had no idea what to make of it until the lights came up and it became suddenly obvious: the theatre was crowded with old short Eastern European-looking people. We had come in during the previews in the dark and hadn't noticed. As I got to the end of our row of seats a woman shuffled by in a faded print sack dress who had a long purple number tattooed on her forearm. "Holy shit," I thought. "No wonder!" This was far from being just another movie to these people; it was PAYBACK TIME!! in living color. I wanted to stop a couple of them and say, "you know, those were just actors," but I didn't have the heart for it.

chapter nine

Then there was the day of the Little Big Shack Bumble-bee Massacre. I don't remember what kept us out of the hay fields—maybe another one of those rainstorms that only happened at night—but one beautiful morning Roland smiled his beautiful smile and said, "Boys, I've got a little chore for you."

Just across the driveway from the barn sat several small old sheds in various stages of disrepair. The Boss had decided there was a good job here to keep the help busy on this particular day so he walked us over to one of them.

"Easy morning, gentlemen," he said. "I just want you to grab some tools and tear this shed down. We haven't put anything in her in years; maybe we can find some use for the wood next winter."

While we were standing there in the July sunlight thinking that this would be a nice change of pace from the usual routine, the largest bumble bee in the continental United States tried to land on Roland's nose. Rol didn't miss a beat. Just as he had done with the wasp that made the painters union so nervous a few weeks before, he casually reached out, grabbed that flying fortress, flicked it's head off and tossed it aside.

"Hello, Mr. Bumble," he said. Then he walked away smiling, saying over his shoulder, "There might be a few more of those things in that old lumber but they shouldn't bother you."

Bother us? Holy Christ it was their Home: more like their Palace. As we started to pull a few boards off the nearest wall, several of the deceased's former roommates rose up to argue about our intentions. Within minutes it became clear that not only the biggest bumble bees in history called the Catskills their home, there were at least two other distinct lesser species of 'Mr. Bumble' living in these old sheds, and none of them liked us. We retreated. In fact, we pulled back all the way to the farm house in disarray. Rolly had disappeared so we begged Faye for help. She said she understood our hesitation but the thing had to come down. The hired hands evidently looked so desperate that she took pity on us and went into the basement and came out with two tall spray cans of Black Death or something like it, recommending that we use them sparingly because it was all she had left.

Going back 'out there' took raw nerve. George suggested we face this thing like men.

"Let's pretend we're at the Alamo and Colonel Travis has just ordered us to go outside the walls and burn those shacks between La Villita and that fence Davy Crockett and his Tennessee boys had to defend. Remember that? That took guts."

"They had guns," I said.

"You're right. We need more weapons—some back up if this spray shit doesn't work."

So we armed ourselves with sticks about the size and heft of baseball bats, took some deep breaths and returned to face the enemy.

The thing I remember most about the war was how loud those big boys were. The strategy called for one of us to pull boards while the other watched his back. This worked for a while but soon we were in a fight for our lives. We were in the Alamo, alright, but now back to back, just like Fess Parker and Georgie Russell taking on the Mexicans one by one as they came over the walls at the end of the Walt Disney movie we were suckled on. The big ones were the meanest, no matter what anybody tells you, or maybe just more terrifying. Have you ever had a giant bee come right up into your face with intent to kill making a noise like a B-17? We learned that if you could keep the spray from the can on one of the monsters directly, it would stop maybe a foot away from your head...he would hang there for an awful moment before it killed him and then he would fall out of the sky at your feet. Thank God. But they just kept coming.

The battle raged off and on for over an hour with one of us manning a can, nursing the ammunition, and the other popping flankers out of the air with a club. When the spray ran out it was hand to hand. I will say this about the biggest Bumbles: they were game. You had to admire their courage. They were also a lot easier to hit than the other two kinds. From time to time the bees would suddenly vanish—disappearing to regroup, I suppose—and we would rip out more wood. I swear when they came back at us you could hear them before you would see them, giving us those few precious terrifying seconds to grasp our weapons and brace for the next wave. Once we started whapping them again the fear would recede. Too busy to think; just line one up and pray you didn't miss more than once or twice. As we staggered out of the killing zone for the last time, Roland came up on his tractor.

"Well I see you've got it pretty much leveled," he said. "Good. Anybody get nominated?" Amazingly enough, no one had. He seemed pleased.

The Boss, as I said before, only really lost his temper twice that whole summer. And the second time I think he was more mad at the world in general or maybe the obstacles farming in particular throws your way, than at any of us. We were picking up bales on the one big field he owned across the main road, way up on top of it with a nearly full load of hay when it happened. Whoever was stacking the bales on the wagon had inadvertently gotten them on too loosely packed—which was easy enough to do on a hillside with two guys constantly winging them up at you, especially if one of them was Guzzy. The rig was stopped on a steep angle, and thank God no one was in the way, when most of that full load suddenly decided to slump right off of the wagon and back out onto the field. Of course, just at that moment here comes Roland on his little gray Ford tractor from out of nowhere. We all felt terribly guilty, (although I have to think this kind of thing had happened on a dairy farm before), and stood there looking sheepish as Rol dismounted to survey the damage. A disaster of this magnitude threatened to sabotage a good piece of an afternoon's work and throw his well-tuned and mysterious schedule into turmoil. He gave that spilled hay a long angry stare, then looked up at the four of us.

"Farts," he said loudly. "Balls."

"Shits," he added almost as an afterthought as he turned away, and then he got back up on his tractor and puttered off, leaving us laughing there on that hillside. God, I loved that man.

There was another moment of great peril (for me, anyway) that occurred around this time. A group of us had gone down to a trailer park I didn't know existed, to meet a friend we didn't know existed. He was a nice enough guy, but we never hit it off—probably because one of his visitors (I think it was my brother,) needing to throw up suddenly, had done so in his mother's laundry basket which just happened to be handy. Whoa. Not wanting to extend our stay, several of us went out for some fresh air and started walking down the dark road nearby. For some reason—'it was my own stupidity what done it' they say in the Catskills—when the lights of a car suddenly appeared we all panicked and ran off the road to hide. I was leading this ill-conceived charge into the bushes on the right when two things happened all at once. Realizing even in the darkness that there was a drop-off of some kind directly in front, I came to a sudden halt. The other thing that happened was that George, not seeing me stop, plowed into me from behind and we both sailed off into the night to land hard on a large briar bush just below.

"Holy Shit," I muttered.

"What the hell just happened?" George asked.

"You just landed on top of me on a tree" I said.

"Oh...well...thanks for breaking my fall," he said politely.

We untangled ourselves and got out of there, laughing, amazed that neither one of us had been maimed or killed. In fact, everybody thought it was funny, especially since there had been no need whatsoever to panic and run from anything, but I was banged up pretty good. Just scratches and bruises, it turned out to be a harbinger of things to come the very next evening—a warm up act, if you will, but there was no way of knowing that at the time. Don't be too hard on my brother for trying to kill me or even for ralphing into an unfortunately placed basket in the trailer. I had been guilty of a far worse breach of decorum a few weeks earlier. In the middle of the night George woke to some strange sounds and found me on the floor of our bedroom kneeling in front of a box filled with Wee Wee's high school cheerleading mementos puking my guts out directly into it.

Heroes for hire indeed.

The dark entrance to the cavernous "mows".

A little storage shack just to its left. That old barn had so many
secret hidden rooms in or attached to it that I never even
found a couple of them until years later.

chapter ten

"Be always sure you're right, then Go Ahead."

David Crockett said that.

The night after our little space walk George decided he just had to go visit Claire down in Poughkeepsie where she was in nursing school, and enlisted Guz and John and I for a quick road trip. The idea that she might have little nursey friends who were dying to meet some dashing farm hands had occurred to me, but when we got down there Claire came out of the old brick dorm by herself and just hung out with us on the front lawn. No night nurse for the weary. The sweethearts went off to one side leaving the rest of us cooling our heels, when the strangest thing happened. One of those heels, the one on my right shoe, a smooth brown loafer I was wearing without socks, fell off. It just fell off; no explanation. At the time, it didn't seem like a big deal, just weird. I thought I could make it home barefooted easily enough, but I should have known better. The last time I had been barefoot outdoors was just before the run-in with Doctor Fairbairn and the special delivery we shared in the barn. This evening we were on our way to another Rendez-vous with Destiny and here I was going to show up without shoes on...again.

To her credit, Claire was a classic mountain girl—beautiful, but open and friendly to all of us—not hung up on herself like so many of the really pretty girls in Mount Lebanon had been. Maybe it's a big school thing: a couple of hundred half-wit adolescent boys hitting on them and making such a big fuss all the time that by ninth or tenth grade they are ruined. If you are not on the football team just forget it. She, however, was confident and cheerful and funny and it made me sick that she didn't have a twin sister.

After dark, we said goodbye to her and headed up the Thruway to the Kingston-Pine Hill exit and Route 28 that sends you winding back up into the mountains. The night was young and there was a general thirst so George pulled the Chevy into the parking lot of The Retreat, a pizza place/tavern perched on a hillside about half way up the first long climb out of Kingston. It seemed like a nice enough bar, if a bit crowded and noisy. There were some couples at the bar and a long table near the door filled with a group of especially loud young men who Guzzy figured were counselors from a nearby summer camp out for a howl. The four of us found a table off to the side and settled in for a pizza and a pitcher of Genny.

So far so good, and we were waiting for our change when a refugee from the loud guys table—there had to be eight or nine of them—lurched by us on his way out of the men's room. One of his friends yelled out to him loud enough for everyone in the establishment to hear plainly.

"Hey Jimmy! You forgot to wipe your ass!"

This was apparently the funniest thing these boys had ever heard and they were still laughing about it as we got up to leave, but something about it really bothered me. And then something shifted inside me. I suddenly knew that for the first time in my life I needed to take a stand (alongside Errol Flynn and Fess Parker—Robin and Davy) for what was just and right and decent in the world. I had to or I would always be ashamed of myself. Having reached that crossroads, I proceeded (from any objective rational viewpoint) to do the single dumbest thing I've ever done in my life. After John V.B., Guzzy and George had gone out the door, I stopped at the head of the offending table to have a word with them.

"Gentlemen," I said quietly to the upturned faces going down either side, "I believe you owe the women in this establishment an apology."

Now I happened to be wearing one of my favorite shirts that night, an old long-sleeved pin striped work shirt some forgotten gas station attendant had Good Willed me. It had a white patch above the left pocket with the word, "ESSO" written in bold red letters. A sudden hush fell over the multitude and I clearly remember two rows of drunken faces staring up at me in disbelief. For a long moment, no one said anything. Then the biggest guy in the group, sitting two chairs down on the right, settled on the appropriate response.

"I Hate ESSO," he snarled.

With that, he threw his half full beer all over me. That really got them going. As the laughter subsided, I sheepishly began to stammer out some kind of apology to put them off while my hand slowly closed around a full mug on the table in front of me and I suddenly threw the beer in it directly into the big one's ugly face just to return the favor.

Kowabunga, Buffalo Bob. That table simply erupted. A frantic wave of pissed-off counselors reared up on its hind legs and broke over me. I put both hands up in front of my face to ward off the flying fists and at first the crush seemed to work in my favor because there were so many of them I guess they got in each others' way and I kept my feet. But one of them managed to smack me in the left side of the head with a heavy beer mug and it sent me to my knees. Now I was really fucked.

And then the cavalry arrived. Unknown to me, and unnoticed by my attackers, George had glanced back into the bar on the way out, happened to see me pause to deliver my lecture on common courtesy, and wisely touched Guzzy's shoulder. They were waiting in the shadows just outside the door praying I wouldn't do anything stupid when of course I did and all hell broke loose. Both said later that they had the easy part. Everyone was so intent on getting to me the two of them simply waded in and started tapping people on the shoulder and hitting them in the face as hard as they could when they turned around to see who was there. In the confusion, I was able to get to my feet and something happened that was so right out of a Hollywood western I still find it hard to believe. My brother had quickly hammered his way to my side and as I stood up we found ourselves together and instinctively we went back to back. For a crazy surreal moment it all seemed to stop. Hell, it did stop. I can't explain it but everyone and everything paused for a heartbeat and George and I actually had time to look at each other out of the corner of our eyes and start to laugh at the bumblebee absurdity of it all. Then the madness clicked back in; everything became a roaring haze again, hard to make sense of it, but out of that roar the big brute came barreling in on me.

My snarling friend (who wasn't all that tall, but by God he was wide) came in low from the left meaning to tackle me but in the press couldn't get a decent running start and so only lurched against me head first. It was a generous gift. I wasn't mad at all, just scared close enough to death to know I had to keep hitting people if I wanted to survive, so I grabbed his hair in my left hand and whacked his face as hard and as fast as I could with my right fist several times and shoved him down to the floor.

Looking around for George, I got a quick glimpse of Guzzy picking one of the smaller dudes right up in the air by his shirt and cocking his arm, but then somebody I never even saw cracked me in the back of the head and I went down again.[17] This time, before I could get up I felt someone grab MY hair with two hands and start to pull me along the floor. I knew immediately that it had to be Bluto back for revenge and had time to think: "Jesus, this guy's immortal; he won't stay down," but then the hands holding my hair suddenly let go. My brother had seen him dragging me and jumped in front of the great bastard and there was a long lovely moment where he had time to center all that power gathered from hours of lifting heavy milking cans and throwing hay bales, not to mention rowing freshman crew at Harvard, and he let that big boy have it square in his already bloodied nose. George said the look on that bully's face of amazed sorrow just before the punch landed was something he would always cherish.

The rest of my assailants had retreated out into the parking lot, so Guz was free to top things off and he caught "I hate Esso" staggering away from George's shot, spun him around and hit him so hard that he literally flew out the front door. I never got to see any of this. Shortly after I felt those big hands let go of my hair an even stronger presence

---

17. Hard to put a footnote in the middle of a fistfight, but George said later he saw Guz hit that little fuck and that the guy went sailing through the air into the next room and crashed against a jukebox shattering the face of it. Right out of an Errol Flynn western. (The epic saloon fights in San Antonio and Dodge City come to mind, minus the jukebox). Not surprisingly, Guzzy never talked much about his role in this business. Suffice it to say, he and my twin brother saved my life by coming back through that door.

put a gigantic arm around my head and held me tight—head locked between a bulging forearm and a monstrous bicep. I couldn't see that either of course but I didn't need to. I went limp. It was over. Whatever was holding me in its massive grip could crush me like a walnut if it chose to, so I decided to relax and concentrate on not crying. The pressure on my skull was enormous.

When George and Guzzy turned back into the wreckage of what had only minutes before been a quiet restaurant they were dismayed to see Paul Bunyan glaring at them with me dangling helplessly at his side. It really was him: great dark bushy beard, red plaid lumberjack shirt; he was the biggest man they had ever seen. What to do? Thank God George had recently held down major roles in two plays senior year of high school, because he now saw an opening for a beautiful dramatic moment. Without missing a beat, he jumped up on one of the few remaining upright chairs and addressed the crowd.

"Everybody listen," he said. "We didn't start this fight. My brother there was only standing up for the honor of the women in this place and those drunken animals attacked him because he had the courage to defend that honor when no one else would."

Or words to that effect. I couldn't really hear anything clearly but I could feel the hideous pressure slowly relaxing and finally releasing me altogether. I sat there on the floor resting my head against a huge leg and glanced furtively up at this giant of a man who seemed to be listening intently to something important. Just then a young stranger came through the front door.

"They're waiting for you in the parking lot," he said. "Two more cars have shown up. Must be from their camp."

"Well that tears it," George said quickly. "We're going out there. Who is with us?"

A man standing way off in the corner with his wife or girlfriend who he had evidently been shielding from the mayhem, stepped out and said: "I'll go with you." I got to my feet and looked up again at Mr. Bunyan who smiled down at me. Given the way we'd met, I found that smile rather encouraging.

"I'm with you," he said quietly.

It seemed like the whole world had changed but in real time the fight couldn't have lasted very long. In fact, John V.B., as stalwart a companion as one could ask for, never even got involved in it. He was all the way to the car before noticing he was alone and only wandered back into the Retreat during George's fabulous Sermon on the Mount. (He did say on the way home that he had admired the style and tone of the speech.)

Now as Guz and I led our new brigade out into the soft glare of the parking lot lights we could see two things right away. There were, in fact, quite a few new faces in front of us and, even more discouraging, the Original Gorilla was back on his feet leading the pack our way. I couldn't believe it. His face was a terrible mess. That guy, however, had grit, and he walked right up to us before our troops behind could even clear the door. What happened next has always amazed me and I still don't fully understand the physics of it.

"Move or I'll move you," he said to Guzzy and then hit him full in the face.

The blow made a sickening thud. Before anyone else moved a muscle, Guz gave a little shrug of annoyance—the same gesture Steve Reeves used in the old Hercules movies when perplexed—reached out, grabbed Bigfoot by the neck and shoulders, swung him around in some kind of 'Full Nelson' and had him hanging limp facing his friends. He was completely helpless, and wearing what amounted to a sheepish grin on his battered face. In a flash, George saw another opening for diplomacy and stepped in between the hostile armies.

"If you want your friend here back, it's over," he shouted. "It's as simple as that."

And it was.

The crowed of angry councelors hesitated for a moment, and then parted to make way for us. As we walked slowly to the car, one of our recent enemies asked, "Why don't you come back in and have a beer?"

"No thanks," somebody replied, not wishing to see again the unholy wreckage we had helped create. As we opened the doors to the little car, another voice rang out from the dark crowd.

"Hey! Where are you guys from?"

"The Motor City!" George yelled back.

It was a fitting answer from our new spokesman; a last defiant statement ringing in the night air. And so we got in the Chevelle and drove away from the Retreat. After a couple of minutes of silence, John V.B. turned to George.

"Why did you say Detroit?" he asked.

"I don't know," George replied. "It sounded good though, didn't it? I sure as hell didn't want to tell them we were from Margaretville. They might come looking for us to help pay for that fucking mess."

Blessed are the losers, for they shall inherit the damages.

Speaking of damages, this is the little ancient window where
the transistor radio that played the muzak lived.
Really a very trippy view of an outbuilding and the farm house
up above. Never noticed it while milking.

chapter eleven

The next morning we were working a field just below the farmhouse and barn, down to the left of the long driveway as you were coming in. I remember it because it was alfalfa, which is this thick weird dark green stuff that had to be treated pretty much like hay. And I remember walking past John V.B. that morning as he stood at the foot of a ladder contemplating the painter's life.

"Why if it isn't Cassius Clay," he said smiling as I ambled past. Aside from a series of what appeared to be teeth marks across the swollen knuckles on my right hand, and a major lump on one side of my head, the whole affair from the night before already seemed like some strange dream, but John's greeting did make me smile. Later that evening, Mountain, who was a little put off that he'd missed the Battle of the Retreat, asked if we had heard a new song on the radio called *A Boy Named Sue*, by Johnny Cash.

"You guys are going to love it," he said. "There's a line in there about breaking chairs and 'kickin' and a gouging' in the mud and the blood and the beer.'"

"I don't think they're going to play it in the barn," I said. "The cows wouldn't care to hear about that."

It was a summer to be listening to the radio, *A Boy Named Sue* or not. Sadly, we only got snatches of AM radio while driving around at night, and whatever made it on the juke boxes of various bars. It was a strange brew. You could hear songs by Creedence (Green River came out in August), or Hendricks, Janis, The Doors, The Who, mixed up with all kinds of painful pop like *In the Year 2525*, or *Dizzy*, by Tommy Roe. Or *Sugar* (fucking) *Sugar* by The Archies. So radio was the typical crap shoot we took for granted at the time. But imagine walking into a bar on a warm summer night and hearing *Lay Lady Lay* for the first time. Whoa. When that song was playing in Lange's the universe seemed meaningful. Maybe even friendly.

Rufus must have sensed I was having good thoughts like these too often because about then he did something to me that was impressive even for him. For some reason one afternoon there were no cows loitering around the back of the barn waiting to get milked. Roland scratched his head, as he liked to do, while looking down at the ground.

"Well...it probably means they wandered up the hill too far and got a little lost. Take Rufus with you and bring them down. It should be alright...find 'em and he'll do the rest—he enjoys showing them who's in charge."

"They can actually get lost on their own farm?" I asked innocently. "The whole herd?"

"Cows are easily distracted, John. You must have noticed that by now. Just have Rufus get them started down-hill and they'll find the barn easy enough."

So off we went, Rufus and I. Though he seemed happy, I still had my doubts and the farther up the mountain we hiked the more I wondered what could have possibly gone wrong. We found them, eventually, way up near the top, and it was the damnedest thing. Roland was right: they were lost in the woods. By that I mean they had evidently drifted out of a meadow into a nearby grove of trees and gotten hopelessly confused. I know this sounds ridiculous but having the trees all around somehow convinced them all that further movement was impossible.

I was laughing at first. The little bit of cow psychology I had dabbled in led me to believe that, while occasionally they may show evidence of distinct personality traits, dairy cows are both incredibly curious and unbelievably stupid. For instance, they will walk across a big field to see what you are up to on the other side of a fence and then just stand there staring at you as if they can't remember why they came over.

Animated conversation between two of them after doing this:

Cow I: "Moooooo....uh....what's he doing?"

Cow II: "Uh...I dunno."

Two minutes of hard staring later:

Cow I: "Where are we?"

Cow II: "Uh...I du....what's he doing?....moooooo."

Which is all well and good and amusing in the abstract, but how do you explain to a large group of such beings that it's time for moving back down hill to the barn when you realize that they are so petrified by seeing tree creatures all around them that they absolutely refuse to budge one way or the other? And my comrade, the skilled Australian Shepherd, bred down through the generations to herd cows? Unbelievably, Rufus walked to the center of a small clearing just above the trees where the girls were stuck and sat down on his haunches. He sat down there and looked over at me as if to say: "What now, city boy?" That struck me as a bit surreal so I walked out of the grove to talk to him. I said something like this.

"Rufus, you fuck. What are you doing? Bark at these goddamned beasts or something. Drive them the hell down the hill!"

But he just sat there watching me. Not quite laughing like he had done after he goosed Big Red and sent me flying in the barn, but obviously amused by my impotence.

"For Christ's sake, Rufus, don't do this to me," I pleaded.

It didn't work. He would not budge, so I swore at him some more and walked back into the trees and tried to imagine what Roland would do in this ridiculous situation. Nothing came to mind. After some soul searching, a little well-directed violence seemed like the only way out of the quagmire. I was uncertain what the local courts would have to say about beating these dumb brutes and I had never seen the Boss lose his temper and assault one. But I was at the end of my rope and going all the way back down the mountain to ask advice seemed like a very bad idea.

So I did what I had to do. I picked a cow who was at the lower edge of the woods, pointing in the right direction, and elected her the new leader. Then I found a suitable weapon of persuasion—a stick, more like a small four-foot log—and smacked the back end of that cow hard. Nothing happened. Frustrated as I was, and figuring I had crossed the line now and what the hell, I whacked her again several times while screaming at her and...God Be Praised! The poor critter staggered forward out into the open. That's all it took. As soon as the 'Chosen One' made a few purposeful steps, the rest immediately began to move following her lead, and the whole herd slowly migrated out of the trees and started down the path. At this marvelous moment, Rufus came back to life and started dashing back and forth professionally nipping ankles and driving the pack like he was supposed to.

All the way back down the hill I tried to make sense of what had happened with the cows and the dog and what to tell Roland. I was afraid that beating a cow with a big stick might be considered a mortal sin, but the truth was so strange and funny that I decided to go with it. Sure enough, it didn't faze him. He chuckled for a moment about Rufus and then started the evening milking and we were quickly back into the timeless rhythm of that job as if nothing extraordinary had happened at all. George was greatly impressed by Rufus' decision to play the innocent bystander.

"That bastard may yet prove to be Che Guevara," he said. "Maybe we're mixed up on the dates."

On or about July 20th something happened that demanded the attention of nearly the whole world, but I swear that if it had not occurred on a Sunday we would only have learned about it later from the *Daily News*, or maybe Gram at supper. While we were busy being 'heroes for hire' some real bona fides were flying to the moon and thinking about landing on it. Other than in Jules Verne's twisted imagination—and the 50's movie version of *From the Earth to the Moon* has got to stand as the film with the worst special effects ever (excepting any Saturday morning episode of *Captain Video*)—no one had really tried this stunt before.

Because it was a Sunday, many of us converged in the living room of Rolly's other younger brother, Bob, a sweetheart Van Benschoten with beautiful wavy white hair and the family twinkle in his eyes, who worked for the forestry service and owned a house in Margaretville. We were all there holding our breath when they landed and back again some hours later when they popped the hatch and Armstrong's crackling voice announced his "one small step." There were no dry eyes in that living room.[18]

Occasionally, I should admit, there were moments when farming seemed at least as dangerous as going to the moon. Besides the veterinary lesson, the runaway tractor, a near-death napping experience and the flying fists, my closest brush with death that summer had to be early on when I came down with a dose of what my older brothers would have called "The Terminal Grinds." One morning while riding on a tractor near the farmhouse, I suddenly had an overwhelming urge to get off that tractor, inside that farmhouse and into the bathroom. As I got down and started hobbling slowly towards the back door it felt like one of two things was about to happen very soon: I was either going to die or void myself so horribly in public that I might as well be dead.

Here's a fun fact I learned later while reading Steven Ambrose's *Custer and Crazy Horse*. More men died of

---

18. Many years later there has been some serious speculation that we were all had, and that while the twins were on a real farm dealing with real cow shit those other boys were on location somewhere in Nevada. My older brother Larry, who loves these kinds of alternate explanations for just about anything you can think of that our government has ever done, had a charming moment connected with this theory. He watched the landing with some friends in the oldest house in El Paso, Texas (where he was in Army "Intelligence" at Fort Bliss). A little later in a bar, he happened to see a hundred-year-old-plus ex slave on the TV who argued, convincingly, "A'in no body gon' to no moon." The old man may have been right, but I still hold out the hope that our patriotic tears were not shed in vain.

looseness of the bowels in the Civil War than ever died from bullets.[19] Had I been aware of that concept in 1969, the dread term, "amoebic dysentery" would have come to mind and I might have given up and collapsed right there in the driveway, but in my ignorance, I staggered on. It was only when I reached the upstairs bathroom a few minutes later that I thought for certain I was a goner.

Something in the water? Evidently. And that little tiny something wanted to kill me in the worst way. "In the worst way" is not an exaggeration here. For nearly twenty-four hours I shuffled miserably about my work expecting Robert Redford to show up at any moment dressed like a policeman and lead me away. "Here...take my hand. Trust me."[20] I would have gone with him without an argument. I refused to eat or drink much of anything because it seemed like a waste of time or even worse, an encouragement to whatever dread-

---

19. Damn! Figured if this went far enough there might be a need for another genuine footnote. Here it is in all its technical glory.

Ambrose, Steven. *Crazy Horse and Custer: The Parallel Lives of Two American Warriors.* New York: Anchor, 1975. pp. 26. (Alright, it's not completely genuine. Anchor actually only printed a soft-cover version in 2003—don't know the original publisher—and I made up the page number because I lost the book years ago, but he said it in there somewhere.)

20. "Nothing in the Dark," *The Twilight Zone* (Season 3, Episode 16). Written by George Clayton Johnson. (Rod Serling, Creator.) Featuring Gladys Cooper. Originally aired 5 January, 1962. This is a famous episode where an elderly woman, scared of dying, refuses to go outside of her tiny dark apartment. One day a wounded policeman appears at her door begging for help and she lets him in. Mistake. He is, of course, Death, played by an impossibly handsome (and then largely unknown) Redford. [On a major footnote roll now.]

ful beast was living inside of me. Then, as quickly as it came on, it was over, and I knew I would live. The sky was bluer, the hay smelled sweeter, the bales felt lighter. That evening in the kitchen, even the aroma of burned-ass-of-cow seemed more like an old friend than a new enemy.

And speaking of danger and death, remember my uncertainty about the use of force in human/bovine relationships? One hot afternoon in early August Roland put that question to rest. It was that little bitch, Ginger, of course, who crossed the line. The Boss was milking her and around the third or fourth time she kicked off the milking machine hard, (which was her specialty) he jumped back and yelled something like this: "So that's it, is it?" She was second in from the big door where the cows came in and their shit went out and old Rol only had to move a couple of feet for a tool. He chose a big flat manure shovel and swung that thing high over his head and then down, cracking her square across the back with it. WHAM!! For her part, Ginger staggered forward against the contraption holding her neck in place and seemed to slump into a posture of complete submission.

"Oh, that was swell. Hit her again," I said out loud. George, who hated her even more than I did, was also cheering him on from the other end of the line. But Roland only put the shovel back against the wall and calmly re-attached the milker. Of all the seemingly endless hours I spent in the barn that summer, this one shining moment stands alone. We were privileged to witness the law of karma playing out right before our eyes. It was a rare glimpse of Divine Retribution: a descending blow from His Terrible Swift Sword, delivered well and true by the stout heart and strong arms of one of the chosen people of God. Amen.

Very close to the scene of that crime.

chapter twelve

(Mr. Toad Goes to Woodstock)

Of all the good luck we experienced on the farm that summer there was one bit of timing that capped it all. The end of "first cutting," when all the hay in all the available fields has been successfully packed away in the mows, calls for a moment of celebration. Of course the work doesn't stop, (the cows don't know the difference), and there will be a "second cutting" of all the grass that has had a chance to grow back since June and early July in many fields, but there is a feeling of accomplishment and a pause to take stock. It just happened to land near the end of the second week of August and that night at dinner Roland got out some Canadian Club and ginger ale and poured a drink all around—John and Guz were invited—for his haying crew. The Boss was all smiles and freely gave his blessing to the start of a three-day vacation for his boys. Just on the chance that we might be able to get free, the four of us, and Mountain and Clarke, previously sent away for tickets to a concert that was being held nearby. They cost something like eight dollars a day which amounted to a good piece of a weeks' wages—but three days of peace, love and music was promised and, as Steve McQueen says in *The Magnificent Seven*, "...it seemed like a good idea at the time."

I think it was Mountain who talked the rest of us into going but once again it was Clarke and his dad, Roswell, who helped make it happen. Clarke pulled into the farm right after dinner in the Wagoneer and we all piled in. Roz had forgiven us for our letter to the News, (I think), and I hope he eventually forgave us for what took place next because the first stop was Bussy's store in Margaretville to put in supplies, and it was the editor's good credit that once again stocked our lunar module with food and beer for the trip. To this day I have no idea how to get to Max Yasgur's farm. You don't worry about navigational skills when you are in the back of a Jeep starting a much-needed vacation with your fist wrapped around a quart of Budweiser. Young Sanford procured several cases of quarts and we naively assumed this would last us into the weekend.

As we drove into that good night the anticipation of seeing live music was palpable, especially for my brother and I who were the only musicians in the crew, at least as far as anyone would admit. I clearly remember the moment I started playing drums. It was in Miss Cratty's first grade class in Crafton. She was a man-mountain of a woman with a good moustache and a bad temper. Caught between long stretches of boredom and short bursts of terror—an environment that would have been a good place to begin to prepare for a career in the military as well—we were always on the lookout for new ways to pass the time. One morning I decided that if I could only make my tiny little right hand work a certain way, dropping my fingers on the desk from left to right, it would make a cool noise. Sort of like the sound the galloping horses made in the western movies on TV every Saturday morning starting at eight o'clock sharp. It wasn't easy, but there was plenty of time to practice and after maybe twenty minutes I scored a breakthrough. Bdddrrrum-

mmm, bdddrrummmm, bdddrrummm. Try it: it's fun. Between the sense of accomplishment and the rhythm of the
thing I was hooked. By the end of the morning I thought of
myself as a drummer. Pretty soon, I was marching around
our little house with a pair of chopsticks beating the hell
out of a cookie tin tied around my waist by a bathrobe belt.
My twin, meanwhile, seemed to take to the piano lessons
Mother Kincheloe heroically gave all of her children with
a much better attitude than I did, and after our Big Brother
Bob came back from Harvard with an acoustic guitar one
winter, George was as lost to the Peter Pan world of wanting
to be a musician as I was.

We were performing folk songs in front of audiences by
the age of twelve. Have you ever played a Girl Scout Mother/
Daughter luncheon without a microphone? The noise they
made eating drowned us out. We actually stopped in the
middle of a song because we started laughing too hard to
sing, and the fact that nobody seemed to notice as they furi-
ously gorged themselves on the roasted chicken was even
funnier. By senior year of high-school we were slugging it
out in city-wide "Battle of the Bands" in a rock group called
The Quaker Blues. The band did Paul Revere and the Raiders,
The Kinks, The Byrds and among other things, a song called
Get Together, by an obscure songwriter named Jesse Colin
Young. His neglected solo album had been introduced to us
by our beloved older brother Larry, and the Youngbloods'
Get Together had been a hit (briefly) on the Chicago AM
radio stations we listened to constantly at Conference Point
Camp during the summer of 1967. Nobody in Pittsburgh had
heard this song yet in 1968 so we 'kind of implied' to audiences that it was 'one of ours.' By the end of his first year up
in Cambridge, George had written fifteen or twenty good
songs of his own.

But everybody on the Catskill traveling squad that night loved music and on the way to the Woodstock festival a few were particularly excited about the chance to see The Band, who had played with Dylan and made such an impression with their album, *Big Pink*. And all of us were talking about a brand-new group, Crosby Stills and Nash, refugees from three great bands, the Byrds, the Hollies and The Buffalo Springfield. Everything else would be considered gravy.

George and I realized early on that summer that Mountain liked to sing and it took no time at all to learn that one form of high-quality entertainment was the three of us belting out weird songs from old movies we loved. He taught us a Cossack love song from *Taras Bulba* ('starring?' Yul Brynner) that contained the immortal refrain, "If we drink we will die, if we don't drink we will die, so we'll drink and say What the Hell and Die!" We returned the favor by forcing him to remember the drunken scene in *The Vikings* (with Kirk Douglas and Tony Curtis) where they get off by whipping axes at big-chested blond girls' pigtails. The hit song for us from that film did not have words; it was the melody the dude on the giant horn plays when the Viking ships return to their home fjord. This is a brief but timeless classic we never tired of performing together at odd moments of exuberance, attempting to replicate that funky sound. (Try that too for a good time if you can remember it, but it helps to have six beers in you and some partners.)

Because we lived so near, freeways were unnecessary (thank God), however, it must have been around ten at night when we found ourselves reduced to creeping along some dark country road mired in a gigantic and unexpected traffic jam.

"Jesus, where did all these people come from?" someone said. It was still Thursday evening, the music wasn't
supposed to start until Friday afternoon and we thought
coming in to this little concert the night before meant we
could waltz right in, hand over our tickets and have plenty
of time to set up the big tent we brought along and settle
in for the weekend. Nobody knew how far we were from
the concert site and Clarke was getting impatient behind the
wheel.

"Fuck this business," he was muttering softly over and
over to himself when Guzzy suddenly said, "My lord, it's
Toad."

Many people were already walking along the road around
us making somewhat better time, (and there had been some
discussion in the jeep whether this was a good sign or a
bad one) when Guz looked out the shot gun window to
discover that the heavy-set-nearly-bald-disgruntled guy
plowing along beside us was in fact an old friend of theirs
from Margaretville High—the one and only Mike George,
affectionately known as Toad.

He had a scrawny-looking little guy in a loose tee shirt
trailing along behind him. Guz got out, opened the side
door and said, "I don't know where you think you are going,
Toad, but you might as well climb in with us." I didn't think
much of the idea at first. Toad looked dangerous. Built along
the lines of a beer keg, he had small eyes that darted around
in his face and I could see right away where he got his nickname. The kid with him struck me as an affable enough
cretin; all in all, these two were not a welcome addition to
our tried and tested band of brothers. But beneath Toad's
gruff exterior lurked a comic genius of sorts.

"Jesus Christ! Where have you assholes been?" he grunted as we made room for him and his little shadow. After a few more minutes of frustration with the traffic jam, Clarke spied a dirt road going down off to the right and pulled out of line. At the bottom of a small hill just off the road, he stopped and there was general agreement that this was as good a place as any to sleep. In the morning we would figure out the next step. That step turned out to be so bizarre, so unique a blend of Sanford wackiness and pure Catskill 'go ahead' that I still can't believe it happened.

As the sky began to brighten we crawled out of sleeping bags scattered around the Wagoneer and stood scratching and stretching, feeling pretty lost. Clarke, however, had an idea.

"Guy over there says the festival is right up over this hill here. Come on, let's find out."

So we jumped back on board. I remember looking around thinking: "you're kidding, right?' but Clarke put her in gear, splashed right across a small creek and lurched into the woods on the other side. We were all laughing and yelling as the jeep climbed up a hill through some trees and then came out on a field fairly crowded with people. Our intrepid driver kept her going to the top of the ridge and sure enough there was a dirt road also filled with folks moving mostly one direction so he turned right and we began inching along with the crowd. Unbelievably, we were inside the concert area with our vehicle—tent, sleeping gear, food and all—and when we got to a place where the road started to drop down again, Clarke pulled off to the left and parked on the edge of a big empty field overlooking the natural basin where someone had constructed a huge stage. Waugh.

Everyone scrambled out and up went the tent. It was a beauty, big enough for all of us and solid enough to keep rain out which was a wonderful thing considering all of that rain that only fell at night that summer was about to change its mind. Nature was going to dump all hell on our little group and the several hundred thousand other people who just happened to show up, tickets or not.[21] That first morning, however, the sky was a bright blue and it felt good not being in a barn full of cows. There was this one problem. There were so many goddamned human beings all around us, and evidently more pouring in, that it was breathtaking—disturbing, even. I didn't understand why (exactly) until sometime the next day when I was wandering along the hillside by myself trying to grasp the magnitude of the crowd and suddenly realized two things: I would never ever see that many people in one place again in all my life, and I would never ever feel so utterly alone as in that moment. Once I figured that out, I was fine. It wasn't like leaving was an option. Make the best of it.

But Friday morning none of that mattered as we set up camp and introduced ourselves to our new neighbors who pulled in a little behind us (on vehicles good for eluding traffic jams) and also decided that the edge of this field was an excellent place to stop. Bikers. Scary to look at but friendly enough. They seemed as baffled as the rest of us to find themselves in such an unexpected environment. We hadn't given it too much thought but George and I, at least, had imagined

---

21. I kept mine in my wallet for a couple of years, (un-ripped, because we had flanked whatever ticket booth existed by Clarke's "Mr. Toad's Wild Ride" through the woods) and then gave it away one night to a friendly stranger in a bar who seemed to think it was some kind of holy relic.

this thing was going to be a much smaller affair, along the lines of the Monterey Folk Festival maybe, a few thousand people. Instead it seemed like everyone on the east coast of America had decided to show up here all at once. A strange coincidence related to that had already happened. As we crept along the road earlier, I was leaning out a window and saw someone behind us from my tiny freshman class at Williams, a tall guy with a black beard named Paul—from Massachusetts, I think. That seemed unlikely in all of that mass of humanity, but there he was. I yelled at him and he turned and waved. What were the odds on that? It was just as weird as running across our next-door neighbor from Crafton in front of Old Ironsides at the Boston wharf while on vacation with our family as kids. While that was amazing, and he was happy to greet our folks, I don't think he cared much for seeing us there as we were occasionally guilty of breaking his windows with well-hit baseballs—a certified longball on the home field. It probably made him nervous about his car in the parking lot.

One of the first things we realized sorting through the gear was that there had been a terrible mistake made with the original beer estimate. It was all gone. Mountain said he would find beer if it killed him and he and Clarke took donations and walked off back down the road towards civilization, or something that would pass for it, looking for a small grocery store that someone swore was out there somewhere. It never occurred to me that they would fail us and they didn't exactly. When those brave boys returned an hour or so later they allowed as how there wasn't a beer to be had anywhere in the vicinity, but knowing there was literally nothing to drink had done the best they could and humped two large boxes of beverages back with them. Our new cache was dismaying to look at: two gallons of warm Rhine wine and two cases of bottles of Ripple 'Pagan Pink.'

"Is this stuff even drinkable?" someone asked, which caused Mountain's right eyebrow to go up at least two inches, and Clarke's head to snap sharply in their direction.

"It better be," Toad muttered as if to himself, but his eyes were squarely on Mountain and he was smiling broadly.

I knew we weren't in New Kingston anymore (or Kansas either) when later that morning, as I walked along the ridge-top road taking in the sights, a long-haired shirtless guy with a dark stringy beard went by me offering items for sale. He had an open cardboard box full of goodies supported by a neck strap and as a special touch, one of those change makers that newsboys used to wear in downtown Pittsburgh on his belt.

"Hashish, mescaline, Fritos... Hashish, mescaline, Fritos..." he was saying over and over in a casual monotone as he walked by hawking his wares. I stopped and gawked at him, but it was just the newly-minted farm boy in me. No one else nearby seemed to find it strange.

In mid-afternoon the word went through camp that the music was going to start soon, so our little band crossed the road, worked our way down the hill toward the stage, and found a spot to spread blankets out. It seemed like a long time before anybody played anything but then that really became the signature of the whole weekend-long show: huge periods of waiting for something to happen, anything at all, while a swarm of roadie creatures crawled around endlessly on the faraway stage at the bottom of the hill.

Finally, Richie Havens came on and he was amazing; the music sounded great and I wouldn't have swapped my seat for any place else in the world. The only thing missing was, as I have mentioned, a cold concoction or two. I was taking it really easy on the wine because it tasted so bad.

Have you ever tasted warm jug Rhine wine? Or Pagan Pink
at any temperature? If not, spare yourself the experience.
We have gone to that hillside and spilled that wine for you.
I guess we didn't really need anything else. The weekend
went by in a kind of daze anyway without the help of major
alcohol or chemicals. It was crazy enough on its own terms.

Believe it or not I had never even tried marihuana at that
point in my life. There had been a group of proto hippies
at Mount Lebanon High who evidently discovered it our
senior year, but they were very secretive and called themselves "The Clan" and seemed to be a bunch of assholes.
Probably they weren't. Certainly, it was around at Williams
that first year but everyone in my entry way was still happily experimenting with the effects of large doses of booze
and no one ever offered me any weed. That was to change
this very weekend when Mountain grabbed me in front of
our tent Saturday afternoon where I had retreated during an
extended performance of some band I didn't care for.

"You have to meet one of our neighbors," he said.
"He's got a teepee." And sure enough, five minutes later
some strange man in a head band is handing me my first
joint inside a teepee at Woodstock. (The only thing I had
ever smoked before were cheap cigars, Swisher Sweets, in
Wisconsin, to be cool.) The smell of the grass was very exot-
ic, even exhilarating because it was illegal and new. I didn't
get stoned at all. But I did have the fleeting thought that if
you put a scene like this in a movie, even then, no one would
believe it—it was just too corny.

Anyway, the performers on Friday, many of them acoustic acts, were coming and going between long waits and
nobody near us seemed to be listening all that closely. It
was enough just to be sitting out on that hillside on blankets
looking around at all the people. We kept shaking our heads

and smiling because it seemed so ridiculous that so many of them had all arrived at the same damn place at the same time. It did not seem real at all.

There was one unforgettable musical moment our group shared that day. Ravi Shankar came on with about fifteen or twenty people in white robes sitting all over the stage on pillows with giant sitars, and proceeded to play ten minutes or so of what sounded like "Prelude to Chaos." Sure enough, he stopped the band, got on the microphone and explained what all the non-music was about.

"Thank you very much; we are so happy to be here," he said, or something to that effect. "We have been tuning up because we want to play well for all of you. Now we will begin our concert." Well, they pitched right into their first number and Guz, J.V.B., Clarke, Mountain, George, me, Toad and Toad jr. all looked at each other and burst out laughing because we realized immediately that there was no discernible difference between what they were playing now and the noise that had preceded the announcement.[22] The rest

---

22. Some years later in Los Angeles I got to watch Mr. Shankar rehearsing on a sound stage with George Harrison and many of the best players in town. It was for a tour they were about to go on and just our luck, Bob Rosenberg, George's splendid roommate at school, had grown up with the drummer for both bands, Andy Newmark. Andy is a great guy and an amazing drummer who admitted when I met him on a break that he had to go to his hotel room every night and try to memorize a recording he was making during the rehearsals of the pure Indian music in the opening act because the rhythms were so complex that he was confused most of the time. No doubt, they were playing astounding music at Woodstock as well. We just didn't get it at all. Bob actually visited us on the farm that summer but the only memory I have from that is of him standing in our bedroom swatting flies all over hell and back. He seemed to think there were a lot of them.

of the music on Friday was surprisingly low-keyed, featuring people like Tim Hardin, Melanie, Arlo Guthrie and Joan Baez. Since George and I had cut our teeth on folk music singing The Kingston Trio, Ian and Sylvia, Peter Paul and Mary and acoustic Dylan, that lineup was just fine. As I said, a lot of people in the crowd didn't pay much attention to the performances, but of course, when you are in something that gigantic you only really get a feel for what is going on with the three or four thousand people right next to you.

The best thing that happened to us on Friday evening started out feeling like the worst. It was raining hard, and we had slipped back up the hill before it started to shelter in our magnificent tent. Suddenly a big man with the festival logo—the dove and guitar thing—on his wet red windbreaker stuck his head through the front flap.

"Alright!" he shouted. "You've all got to move immediately! We are about to start using this field to land helicopters and there is no way you can stay here! It's not safe!"

My initial reaction was just to stare at him in disbelief, and for a long moment nobody said anything. I think it was Mountain who hit upon the perfect response.

"No problem pal. Just tell our neighbors. We'll move as soon as they do."

That poor official went bustling off in the direction of our new biker friends and sure enough, no one ever bothered us with that kind of talk again. They did clear the field behind the tent and land choppers out in the middle of it all weekend, but since Clarke had wisely chosen the front edge of it to camp on, and it would have taken an experienced swat team to budge the biker gang in that storm, we were left alone.

Anonymous / Associated Press.

I RODE INTO NAZARETH
    I WAS FEELING 'BOUT HALF PAST DEAD
I JUST NEED TO FIND A PLACE
    WHERE I CAN LAY MY HEAD.

I SAID, 'MISTER CAN YOU TELL ME
    WHERE A MAN MIGHT FIND A BED ?'
HE JUST SMILED AND AND SHOOK
    MY HAND
        'NO' WAS ALL HE SAID.

— DYLAN

chapter thirteen

Saturday was a beautiful day and the list of bands that played all afternoon and into the night now seems like an impossibility: John Sebastian, Santana, Canned Heat, the Grateful Dead, Creedence Clearwater Revival, Sly and his crazy Family and eventually Janis Joplin followed by the Who. There were many more.

One high point of the afternoon was Country Joe McDonald teaching the crowd his *Feel-Like-I'm-fixing-To-Die Rag.* If there was anything vaguely uniting the enormous mass of young people on that farm, it was disgust with the failed war in Vietnam and all the lies and arrogance the combined administrations of Johnson and Nixon had used to continue it. It seemed like everybody was on that page and was singing along with Joe. "...And it's one two three what are we fighting for? Don't ask me I don't give a damn, next stop is Vietnam...And It's five six seven, open up those pearly gates. There 'aint no time to wonder why, whoopee, we're all going to die." The *Fuck Cheer* was such a crowd pleaser that they brought the Fish back for another set the next day. At least I think they did. Trying to sort out what happened and when wouldn't help this Tall Tale very much. The weekend comes back as a jumble of images, most of them positive. It's funny how clueless I was as far as making sense of it all at the time.

For example, there was a huge hand-painted sign to the left of the stage that read "WEAREONE." It looked just like that. Put it down to lack of sleep or lack of brain cells, but I spent two days wondering what that was supposed to mean. I processed it as "wear-eon-ee," which, of course, was gibberish, but fortunately I never asked any of the boys what it meant, and sometime Monday morning the mental cloud lifted and I got it. WE ARE ONE.

Well.

Several people told me over the course of the next year or two that "the mob of unwashed hippies at Woodstock had behaved badly and were a disgrace to this country". My own brother, Big Bob the Doctor, even tried to run that by us because that's what the news media told him down in Jacksonville Beach, Florida where he was stationed in the Navy. (That took nearly a case of Busch Beer to straighten out after George and I had hitchhiked down there for spring break our sophomore year.)

What bullshit. The truly amazing thing about that weekend was how nice everybody was to everybody else. It felt like there really wasn't any other choice because we were all packed in there together and the weather made conditions so miserable for so many, that if people had gotten ugly we would all have been in serious trouble. Most of the three hundred thousand or five hundred thousand residents of that potential madhouse—who knows how many were really there—seemed to get that instinctively. It seemed, in fact, that everybody was going out of their way to help people who needed help. We were giving away food to anybody that happened by and asked for it, (thanks to editor Sanford's generosity we had plenty), and so were our neighbors. The bikers were older men (and women) and the ones I talked to were just as amazed and baffled and concerned as we were at the size of the crowd and the potential for disaster.

As far as the age of the crowd goes, I had the impression the whole time that our little band of Catskill Mountain brothers in arms were among the younger people there. Later attempts at recreating this kind of festival often seemed to feature truly mindless sixteen-year-olds doing truly mindless things, but by then it was my turn to have to deal with whatever version of those events the media invented for the nation's entertainment and I may be completely wrong about that.

Saturday afternoon, at least, the weather was fine, the mood was jubilant and the music just kept coming, and the limited trickle of Pagan Pink we rationed out to each other managed to keep fluid levels acceptable. Santana, Creedence, and Sly all put on fine shows. There was so much good music that it was easy to miss at least some of it. Our group used the blanket area as a central rendezvous but everyone drifted back and forth to the campsite occasionally. I remember Toad spending a lot of time there hunched over the fire pit in front of our tent mumbling about hippie lunatics and half-naked women. It was always worthwhile to listen in on what he had to offer. And naturally, many of us chose to strike out on our own to see the sights or locate a porta-potty from time to time. Mountain became convinced that the lake down below us far to the left of the concert hill had to be where unattached women might be found but I don't think he got down there on a serious scout until much later that night.

Late in the evening, by the time Janis Joplin came on, we were all on the hillside and ready for some serious music. Initially disappointed that her group, Big Brother and The

Holding Company, weren't with her—she had a huge band with a horn section, which didn't seem right at first—it only took a song or two to realize how wrong we were. Janis was magnificent. Even now, many years later, it is possible to hear one of her songs come floating through some dark bar and know at once that the combination of her voice and the song she is singing is perfect; nothing can touch the sheer power of it. And that's what it felt like, to me at least, that summer night as she blazed away. There was a general agreement among the New Kingston contingent that her set was one of the high points of all that incredible music.

What came next was certainly in the running for this award. Sometime deep in the night, The Who finally appeared on stage. I remember one of the band announcing that they wanted to try something new and then launching into *Tommy*. It was thrilling. One song after another roared out over us and it all seemed tied together flawlessly. As they neared the climax of that master work, the sky to the east was beginning to light up with the coming dawn and it cast a surreal and perfect glow over the end of an incredible day and night of music. (It seems the Jefferson Airplane came on after the Who, but as much as I loved their songs, we retreated from the hill at the end of *Tommy*.)

There was a certain funky euphoria back at the tent that morning. Those of us still awake all stood around sharing the bottom of a gallon of Rhine wine, not talking much, but everyone knew now that we had wandered into something quite extraordinary, and the bands scheduled for the day ahead promised more fine things to come. Even though the wine had been our only source of liquid refreshment for twenty-four hours, no one had shown any real effects from it. That is until Mountain came storming up the hill that sloped away from our campsite towards the lake just then with a wild look on his face.

"You guys won't believe where I've been!" he shouted. "That lake right down there—everybody swimming naked... naked women all over the place! Holy shit!"

We were all laughing, encouraged that he had discovered such a wonder, but suddenly Toad came charging out of the tent where he had been sound asleep moments before. He was pissed. Mountain thought that this was hilarious and started taunting him. Toad looked back at him with a grimace of pure hatred. Then he walked calmly over to a small pile of firewood someone had dragged in, picked up a fairly hefty stick and turned towards his tormentor.

"Ever hear of War?" he asked. With that he lifted the club over his head and lurched across the campsite swinging it wildly. With a war whoop of his own, Mountain dodged the assault, circled the fire maybe twice, one step ahead of the crazed man trying to kill him, and went running off back down the hill. We could hear his wild laughter as he disappeared into the woods.

Toad triumphant.

Sunday was another interesting day. It began to take on some aspects of a Boy Scout camp out. The part near the end, when everybody feels like a seasoned veteran deep in the middle of a campaign even though you have only been away from the comforts of home a day or two at most. But this was way beyond Boy Scouts. During the morning the news swept through our camp, and, I imagine, the entire crowd, that someone had been killed in a tractor accident in our new 'city' and that one or maybe more babies had been born. "My! People come and go so quickly here," Dorothy had reminded the Munchkins, and this information

certainly lent a new gravity to the situation. I think it was
John V.B. who remarked then that the real wonder was that
twenty or thirty people hadn't been slaughtered for one
reason or another already in a gathering this huge. That
poor guy's death, (never go to sleep under a tractor) actually
underscored the miracle that this thing was working, and
we were a part of it. And the best part was we had no plans
to go anywhere. At least until Monday morning or until they
stopped playing music if it went beyond that.

I don't think they got many bands on during the day
because it seemed like every time they tried it would start
raining again. Of course, we had no idea what the crazy
bastards who put this thing on were going through back
stage. Our universe consisted of the tent site and the little
patch of hillside we staked out every morning. Memories of
that third day are froggy anyways. The lack of real sleep,
the sheer immensity of the crowd and the undeniable weird-
ness of being there at all combined to put a palpable edge
of unreality on everything. It was a good edge, though. I
do recall wandering out into that void of strangers for one
extended and gallant effort to find a place to take a dump.
The woods were just down the hill, but this was somebody's
farm for Christ's sake, even if it could never be the same
after the deluge of humanity, and I wanted to try to do right
by Mr. Yasgur.

Eventually I discovered a line of porta-potties and paid
my respects. You don't want to know what kind of shape
those overworked stations were in. In my travels, I kept hop-
ing that something unexpected, like a root beer popsicle,
might turn up. No luck there, but what I do remember most
vividly was the smell of the hay that some optimistic souls
had scattered around near the latrine area to deal with all the

mud. It had a sharp, sweet, original yet sickening decaying-matter aroma to it that took me by surprise. I thought I had experienced hay in all its possible incarnations already that summer but I was wrong. It was suddenly clear to me that this had to be the smell of the mud pit that Charlton Heston was doing the Moses Two-Step in when he opted to be a Jew instead of the Prince of Egypt in *The Ten Commandments*. Straw and mud trod by the naked feet of untold thousands of unwashed human bodies: we were smelling the air of an ancient civilization in this small corner of the festival and the thought was somehow comforting.[23]

Sometime early Sunday afternoon George and I decided to work our way down the hill and get as close to the stage as we could. It took awhile, but once again people were friendly enough and we were careful not to walk through the middle of groups who had staked out their areas the way we had farther uphill. With some patience, it was possible to get within maybe thirty yards of the band that was playing but that turned out to be a big disappointment as our timing was off. Ten Years After was not one of the groups we had come to see. They could certainly play their in-

---

23. Need to confess to a small Jones here. I love root beer popsicles. Perhaps too much. For example, the very next summer on the way to Polson, Montana to meet up with Crazy Steve Littell, we picked up a beautiful girl hitchhiking by herself out in the middle of Wyoming. She had stunning bright green eyes: at that moment the most beautiful green eyes I had ever seen. Late that night, next to her on a sleeping bag looking up at the endless stars, I tried to convince her that the culmination of Western Civilization—God's ultimate plan for the planet—had been the invention of the root beer popsicle. She didn't buy the theory, she never let me kiss her, and the next morning, with her contacts out, those eyes weren't even green. Shit on a stick.

struments, but that particular genre of 'British-white-boys-play-the-Blues-as-loud-and-fast-as-you-can' was never very appealing to either of us. We stood in a crowd of people who were loving every note, but when one twenty-minute song which featured an endless screaming guitar solo finally ended, the band immediately went off into another one which sounded exactly the same. Unlike the earlier experience with our little brown brothers from India, this wasn't amusing at all. Even worse, we seemed completely out of place amidst thousands of jubilant fans. George and I didn't have to say anything—conversation was out of the question at that volume anyway—we just shrugged our shoulders and sadly trooped back up the hill. We were sad because for a few minutes there it felt like we were so out of it that we didn't even belong at the festival at all. The only thing I ever liked about that band anyway was their name, because as kids we had the Classics Illustrated comic book of *The Three Musketeers* sequel they borrowed it from.

My brother remembers that The Band came on about this time, and that certainly fixed any notions of not belonging. He even remembers being fairly close to them when they started singing *There Aint No More Cane on the Brazos* and being knocked out because that was an obscure folk song we sang as little baby folk singers that no one we knew had ever heard of. I can remember them playing and enjoying it but George was the one in our outfit who was already in awe of this magical group and he was in heaven when they did *Chest Fever.*

Later that afternoon it started to rain again, and back up on the hill five or six of us huddled on our blankets under a large tarp, assuming it couldn't last all that long and that the music would start again soon. At one point, with the rain coming down steadily, Mountain asked Clarke for a cigarette.

"Jesus, Bill, you've smoked every one I brought. Have you ever bought a pack yourself?" he asked.

"Not often," Mountain laughed, "I'd rather borrow them from someone else. Watch this!"

And with that he leaped out from under the tarp into the rain and disappeared. He was back in two or three minutes with a cigarette dangling out of the corner of his mouth and one tucked behind an ear.

"There are some real nice folks just up the hill a bit," he beamed. Guzzy was impressed.

"I believe this boy could get cigarettes off a guy dying of lung cancer," he said.

"I am awfully good," Mountain said as he borrowed Clarke's lighter and fired up a smoke.

Eventually the skies cleared up. All across the vast hillside people were milling about, shaking off wet things, sorting out their gear, wondering how long it would be until something good stirred way down there on the stage. Most of our crew went back up to the tent to poke around hopefully for some food or the stray bottle of Pagan Pink to bring back for when the music would start again. George and I stayed there to watch the blankets and see what might happen next.

Something did. Just then a short guy with wild curly brown hair and a beard, working his way downhill, happened to try his luck in the slippery mud next to our spot by doing a Silver Surfer imitation for three or four feet.

"Hey fella," George said, "that's a great idea. But you can go a lot farther if you put yourself down."

"Yea," I chimed in, "we used to do it out in Wisconsin after a big storm. Trust us, we're professionals."

This suddenly seemed like an ideal place to try something like that so we cleared a run about thirty or forty feet ahead—there was room because everyone was standing around anyway—and we each took a slide in the mud, one at a time. Before long three or four other guys nearby caught the spirit of the thing and joined in. Every time someone went down our course it would get longer and longer as people below moved aside to make room for us. There was no big plan here, simply six or seven young men having fun, and no one else attempted the slide. They probably didn't want to get any dirtier than they already were. But we weren't wallowing in the stuff, just sliding on our hips and staying relatively clean. I don't remember even thinking about that aspect because we had worn nothing but a pair of jeans for two days anyways. Shirts, shoes, socks: all those were left in the tent to try and keep something dry for later, so the idea of getting a little mud on our butts didn't matter.

I took about six good long slides myself and our new group was very supportive, laughing and hollering and helping each other up at the bottom. There was some kind of

background noise building that sounded like a lot of people yelling but in a crowd so vast groups of people were going off like that from time to time all weekend for many reasons. At the end of a great run it hit me that the huge roars we were hearing were for us. George and I were together at the bottom when the realization dawned—many thousands of people watching us all fly down the hill were cheering us on. At that exact moment, we knew without speaking that we were done. Our little mud slide had attracted an audience we never intended and it was time to go. The original small fella was there too, and at least one of the others, so we took them aside and shook hands, said something like, "that was cool man, thanks for the idea," and started back up the hill towards our blankets. It was hard to stop laughing at what had just happened.

"These people are fucking crazy," my brother said as we picked our way up the long slope through the crowd. [24]

---

24. When the movie, *Woodstock* came out, George went to the little college theater near Harvard Square with some friends to see it. In the original version, at least, during one of those scenes where the screen is split into several segments, a camera man panning the crowd picks up on this 'mudslide' and follows a person coming down the hill. As he reaches the bottom, the camera zeroes in very tight. And there I am: standing next to the slider with the biggest grin on my face you ever saw. According to one of his roommates, George jumped up yelling, "Holy shit! That's my brother!" and the audience went wild.

The drawings above are from the latest re-mix of the movie. If you are having trouble appreciating this, it's because Warner Brothers (in a continuing commitment to honor the spirit of "Three Days of Peace, Love and Music") refused to give us permission to use stills from the movie. Way to go Warner Brothers. Or, as my wonderful 5th grade teacher, Miss Cryan, encouraged us to end a letter to a grown-up: "Thank you for your kindness and consideration."

chapter fourteen

Well, that had been a good diversion, but we certainly did not make a big deal out of it at the time. The rest of our friends were curious when we mentioned the fun we had been having but shortly after George and I got back up to our blankets the crowd was moving back in around the area in anticipation of some music and the 'mudslide' was over and seemingly forgotten. The music that night was worth waiting for but once again, the delays between bands seemed to stretch on and on. As an evening mist appeared and settled over the site lending a new dimension to things, we took some old army blankets from the tent and wrapped them around us. For a brief time we were Roman soldiers standing a lonely vigil in the twinkling darkness at the edge of a vast encampment, awaiting an attack by the Gauls. At least that's what I remember feeling like. George didn't say. What we were really waiting for wasn't the Gauls, it was Crosby Stills Nash and Young. Surely, they had to come on soon. If old Julius Caesar had been in charge, however, we would have gotten our asses crucified, because while Blood Sweat and Tears was playing *Spinning Wheel* or something very much like it, the two sentries started to fall asleep while standing up. Twins are good for timing like that. We were literally leaning on each other at this point, taking turns nodding off.

We tried to fight it...desperately shaking our heads and shifting positions, but the strain and excitement of the last three days finally caught up with us and it was a choice of dropping into the muck or bowing our heads in defeat and going back to the dry safety of the tent to sleep. "No way," you might say in astonishment. "How could you do that?" My only answer: "Were you out there?"[25] It's hard to imagine wanting to change anything about that summer— "No Regrets," says Tom Rush in his most beautiful song— but I have always wished I could have had just a few more hours Sunday night on that dark hillside, because those people came on and "scared shitless" or not, evidently played a fantastic set, and it must have been followed by other good acts. If only we could have witnessed the magical moments that brought the music at Woodstock to an end.

---

25. Speaking of both Romans and crucifixion, that's one of my favorite lines from the thousands of old movies absorbed while watching late shows as a kid. *The Robe* is a pretty tacky affair all in all, but who can forget Richard Burton as a Roman centurion staggering around all butt-fucked and befuddled after he wins Jesus' robe while innocently gambling at the foot of the dime-a-dozen crucifixion he's been put in charge of. "Were you out there?" he asks everybody he meets, with a wild-eyed stare. Try this approach sometime when you don't feel like talking to strangers at a party—it really works.

25a. [note to footnote 25.]. The alert reader will have noticed that allusions to religion appear regularly scattered about this narrative. Chalk that up to me being the seventh son (well, fourth really) of the right reverend Dr. Robert Lee Kincheloe, and growing up as a "preacher's kid." Unfortunately, most of these references will seem pretty blasphemous to a devout Christian. In 1969 I would have called myself a Christian, I suppose. Now I tell people (if asked) that I am a Hindu Baptist. This is a wonderful faith that I invented. It allows me to believe that there is good in all religions as well as bad, and to retain a cautious belief in a 'messiah' (Christmas!!) who said "God is love," while also admiring the eastern idea of all life being part of a great mystical unifying force. The coolest thing about being part Hindu is that you get to have gods with elephant heads and lots of extra arms.

Except it didn't. End, that is. No one who was not 'out there' Monday morning would want to believe this, but when I slipped out of the tent into the early light and shuffled back to the top of the hill alone, there was a band still playing. It was performing for a mere fraction of the weekend's multitude. The hill resembled nothing so much as what a used-up battlefield must look like the day after great armies sweep over it and move on—minus all the dead guys, of course. There were pockets of resistance, small groups holding on, and thousands of fans down near the stage, but the great crowd was gone. It didn't seem right, to have music still going, and to top off the strangeness some dude down on the stage in a white fringed outfit was playing the damnedest twisted screaming version of what eventually turned into the Star Spangled Banner on his guitar. I was feeling proud of myself for recognizing that much when I turned to the person standing next to me.

"Who is that?" I asked.

"Jesus, that's fucking Hendrix man," he said gently.

Once more, I felt like an idiot, but this time the feeling that maybe I didn't belong there only lasted a moment. Hendrix was awesome, and by God, even in my own stupidness I did belong here. All of us did. For whatever reasons, we had been here and survived and now it was closing down and nothing like this would ever come around again because you could never really capture it no matter how many people would later try. It couldn't happen again—not like this. So I just shrugged and eventually said, "Thanks man," and stood there watching the greatest guitar player God ever invented as he worked his way through what must have seemed to him (with the absence of the huge crowd) the most disappointing performance of his life. I enjoyed it thoroughly.

Getting out of there was easy. Hell, we had one of the few cars anywhere near the concert itself (because of Clarke's Friday morning heroics) and the place seemed comparatively empty by the time we got packed up. All of us were in a state of semi-euphoria anyway. What could be the rush to get back to the rest of the world after the last three days? There was one moment as we crawled out of the site in the loaded Wagoneer that stands out; one of those flash points that, looking back, said more about what we had all been through than anything else could have.

We were stalled in a line of cars and people, edging our way towards whatever exit that place had, when suddenly there was a state trooper standing by the driver's window. He was young, dirty, short-haired, and looked pissed off. The poor guy was probably exhausted and sick to death of the ordeal of having to watch over this 'hippie love fest' for several days. There was an uncomfortable silence. This was, after all, a Cowboy—the enemy. The silence was broken by, of all things, Mountain, who leaned across Clarke from the shotgun seat and smiled up at the police officer.

"Hey man, can you spare a smoke?" he said.

Everyone in the jeep was stunned by the pure perfect audacity of the question, and so was the cop. He looked at Bill for a long moment as if he had just been asked to spit on The Flag, and then sighed. His face broke into a small tired smile and reaching into his shirt pocket, he pulled out a crumpled pack of Winstons.

"Sure," was all he said, tapping one out and handing it over.

"Thanks, brother," Mountain said smiling again.

"Here...keep the pack," the young trooper replied, and as we lurched away he grinned at all of us and put his right hand up in a peace sign.

Of course we were all starving, and somewhere some-time after we had cleared the mess that had once been Yasgur's farm we stopped in a diner to get some breakfast. I only mention this because of what the teenage waitress said when she brought the menus.

"Wow, you guys were at Woodstock? That's really cool! I hear they had all kinds of music and a mudslide and every-thing!"

A mudslide? That stunned us. Everybody at the table (we had parted ways by then with Toad and his little duckling) looked around and started to smile this one huge identical smile. Of all the things she might have said, how could she know that and why say it to us? I had a strange twinge just then—a brief flash, an intuition of immortality.

"Good God, George," I said softly. "We're cultural icons." That got a good laugh as we turned to the much more impor-tant business of figuring out how much of a beer fund we could still generate for the ride home.

Nobody wanted this weekend to be over. I couldn't im-agine dropping back into an afternoon's work at the farm without some kind of serious debriefing. As the Wagoneer crept slowly into downtown Margaretville, Mountain began singing the *Fixing to Die Rag* Country Joe had taught us and everybody joined in, rolling down the windows so that any civilian on the street could get a full dose of it. Naturally we had to throw in the "Fuck" cheer—"gimme an F! gimme a U!" etc, that had also been part of the show, and this was delivered with gusto while waiting at the town's one stop-light. Clarke understood the need to keep the thing going so he drove up into the hills to a house that his family owned on the edge of a small jewel called Perch Lake and we all went skinny dipping in the cool clean water. I couldn't believe he had never brought us there before but when I asked about this he just grinned.

"Are you crazy?" he said. "My parents put up with a lot, but if they knew I had shown you scoundrels how to find this place they would disown me immediately. Forget this ever happened, if you love me, boys." And so we did.

It didn't take long to drop back into the routine at the Van Benschoten farm. We had had our vacation and it was a beauty but the last weeks of August saw hell-bent-for-leather haying. A bit strange to be back working the fields where we had first learned the ropes, but the grass had grown so fast it was nearly as tall as it was in June. The bales weren't any lighter since a baler by nature does not know the difference (any more than a cow does) between first and second cutting. The days were hot and I remember one scorcher when Wee Wee brought ice-cold lemonade out to us and we took a long break on the lower edge of the field Millers Road ran beside. Standing under the shade of some big maples near an

---

26. Speaking of Wee Wee, I should add that she got to go to Woodstock as well, with several of the older girls from Margaretville, proving (again) how great Roland and Faye were, as none of the other girls her age were allowed to. Their experience took an ugly turn, however, when the parents of the Ghost sicked the state cops on them while they were staying near the site at a friend's house and the Cowboys hauled the Ghost away. Maryanne and Melinda actually ran away from the police and made it into the festival. My favorite part of that story, however, is about Mother Faye. Sick with worry, and convinced (after everyone was gone) that she had made a horrible mistake allowing her lovely young daughter to go to such a potentially dangerous event, she looked out the farmhouse window that Sunday afternoon to see a police car coming up the driveway. "Oh my God, what have I done?" she was asking herself over and over as the officer pulled around back, parked, and slowly got out of the vehicle.

ancient stone wall, there was a general agreement that even beer couldn't beat the taste of that blessed liquid right then on that sweat drenched afternoon.[26]

Roland was glad to have us back and I began to realize how much I would miss him when it was time to head back to school but those last few weeks were so busy there wasn't much time to dwell on the fact that our time was getting short. As for how the Boss felt about us, it wasn't real clear. I had spent the whole summer attempting to live up to his expectations, and hoped we had learned enough to be useful. Rolly privately confessed years later that for a while he wasn't sure whether or not George and I had the right stuff to make the grade as decent farm hands. He happened to be watching me one morning when I took a loaded cow tail at full speed across both eyes. He remembered that I looked up at my tormentor blinking through the tears and without taking my hands off the milking machine, simply rubbed my eyes clean against the soft flank of that cow and went on about my work.

When he got to the foot of the stairs leading to the kitchen door, he looked up at her with a very serious expression and said: "Mam? Would it be alright if I came up here and went coon hunting some evening?"

26a. Sorry for doubling up again. The man who uttered that immortal line was none other than a well-liked local trooper named Joe Hewit. His own quirky Catskill Tall Tale has been captured beautifully in the book, *I Was Corning a Beaver, Like You Do.* by Bill Birns, published by John Burroughs' Woodchuck Lodge and Mountain Arts Media

"I knew right then that you boys would be alright," he eventually told me. It was the highest compliment I have ever been given.

Our night-time forays certainly didn't slow down any. There was one party in someone's backyard in Marga-retville that was memorable for two reasons. The main thing was, I got kissed. It would be great to be able to say that I met a beautiful girl who had been hiding in Europe all summer and came home in time to lend some extra romance to this Tall Tale, but that didn't happen. The sad truth is that Clark's girlfriend Melinda was talking to me in the middle of the yard and he was off somewhere else and I must have said something about what a fine summer it had been with the exception of not having kissed anyone (almost true) and she simply smiled up at me and said, "I can fix that," and suddenly we were kissing. Nobody seemed to mind and it didn't last long or mean anything to her particularly, but I have always been grateful for that small act of human kindness.

A few minutes later Mountain and George and I were singing "...if we drink we will die," partly for the benefit of a group of younger boys who were there. They had been treating us as if we were some kind of mythical characters— legends, whose stories would be told for years to come— and even if I was only imagining that, something happened that probably did get some airplay after we were gone. I was standing off near the edge of the yard in the darkness talking to two of these youngsters when I took a huge swig from a warm can of Rheingold Beer. "Mistake," my throat and stomach said as one, and suddenly I was throwing up into the bushes.

"This will never do," I thought to myself as these kids stood there startled by this rude and embarrassing interruption to our conversation. There was only one possible way to save face at that moment and I seized upon it.

"Sorry gentlemen," I said, wiping my mouth on a sleeve.

"Say, can I borrow that for a second?" I continued, and snatched a beer out of the hand of the nearest boy.

"That kind of thing can make a guy awful thirsty." And with that, I took a long slow drink, said "thanks," and offered it back to him. Understandably, he declined, but my gesture had the desired effect.

It felt good after the wonderful insanity of Woodstock to be back in the barn with the girls and the familiar smells and sounds, milk machines gurgling away, Rufus on his wheelbarrow throne; the muzak seemed almost palatable. No, that's an exaggeration. The cows were so used to us by now that even Ginger, the bitch, behaved herself for the most part. Haying it in those last weeks of August went well. Guzzy, J.V.B., George and I worked hard but smoothly together on those long beautiful afternoons, each one much like the rest. It seemed though that we were bringing in an awesome amount of hay. Near the end, the mows in the barn got so full that we were no longer throwing bales down anymore, but actually stacking them at entry level or above—in some cases pretty high. The Boss was happy. It had been a good summer—a barn full of hay.

The painters were still lurking about the house most mornings as we serviced the tractors in the yard before firing them up to head out to the fields. There is really no way of knowing how much of the old house actually got painted that summer. Guzzy and John still seemed to spend a lot of time looking up, scratching their heads and debating the finer points of ladder placement. Maybe that was just for our entertainment, as they always seemed to be smiling about something. Guz told me years later that his best memory of painting there was when he got mad at a stubborn metal fitting protruding from the siding that wouldn't cooperate and he went down the ladder for a hammer to talk some sense into it. He was banging away at it when Faye came out of the house yelling, "Stop! Stop!" (The rest of us had just sat down to lunch when pictures sitting up on the shelves in the dining room hutch started to come flying off.) That boy was strong.

After an entire summer of trying to get her wayward guests to go to church with her, Gram finally succeeded, but it wasn't on a Sunday morning. Sometime in those last weeks, the village of New Kingston held their first annual 'Whoop De Do' celebration. This was the brain child of the Reverend William Harter and his wife Linda, also a pastor. They were very nice folks who happened to be full of life and optimism and gung ho Protestant-youth-group-type exuberance. The fact that he had gone to Williams was a casual embarrassment to me that George took every opportunity to enjoy. The Whoop De Do consisted of a parade and crafts and local food and a talent show of sorts topping everything off on Saturday night. It was a very big deal to people of all ages in the valley, with the certain exception of anyone our age. Nevertheless, we agreed to go to it with Gram and, much to her delight, actually performed as folk singers to a packed congregation that night in the little village church. I really wish I could remember what songs we sang—a prime candidate would be that song about the Brazos which we did when we were maybe thirteen and had heard The Band play at Woodstock—but I don't recall.

George says now that we "probably threw in whatever half-assed love song" he had recently written but whatever we did I have to think it was a shining moment for our farm family out in the audience.

Our last night at dinner Gram was quiet. She would miss her boys. There was some gentle fun about the caliber of the meat. Faye told a wonderful story about a Jewish gentleman from the city who came to live in Andes, a town not far from her childhood farm. After about a year a local asked him, "So, how do you like Andes?"

"You have a beautiful cemetery," was all he said.

Faye just loved that. I remember thinking that maybe we should stay in and watch TV with Roland, but when George and I talked about it briefly after dinner we realized with what amounted to a start that since our first week there we had gone adventuring every single night that summer. Every night. And so we went out once more to have a goodbye beer with whoever or whatever might present itself.

And then the next (beautiful) morning, it was time to go. Faye wanted a picture and George and I posed with Rufus in the back yard. It's a good photograph. We are not the same skinny suburbanites who crawled tentatively out of their sister's car on that exact spot two and a half months before. Tanned (as far as auburn-haired young men can be), muscular and confident in our jeans and white tee shirts, we are farm boys, and Rufus seems proud to stand with us. The one really baffling thing about the picture is that I am not wearing any shoes.

chapter fifteen

We left the farm that morning after kissing Gram good-bye and hugging Roland and Faye and Mary Ann, pulling slowly down the long driveway past the close-cropped fields, around the tree-lined bend to the little bridge and then pointed Margot's Chevy west towards Pittsburgh. It seemed only fitting that we stop there on the way to Detroit to see Bob and Jane before going back to college, but we must have taken the long way because it was late the next morning when we pulled into Mount Lebanon. The problem was: how to find any of our high school buddies on a week day morning over a year after graduation, so we stopped at a couple of parents' houses with poor results. One old boy, Norm Hickey, father of Warren, the bass player in the Quaker Blues, must have been retired already (perhaps from the stress of raising a teenager in a rock band) because he was home. Norm could barely muster the energy to get out of his living room chair to come to his own front door. When he made it, he looked us over with obvious disdain and simply said, "I don't know where anybody is."

It was only after we stopped in a bar up on Bower Hill Road searching for the fabled grilled chipped ham and melted cheese sandwich George had been hallucinating about since we left the Catskills, that we got a lead. First, there was a rude surprise when the bastards wouldn't serve us a cold one. We ordered a couple out of habit only to be gruffly reminded that Pennsylvania's liquor laws were medieval in scope and intent. Shit howdy. But someone there knew of a house he thought might have been rented by Bob "B" Good and if he hadn't been thrown out yet, some of the boys might be there. Sure enough, when we found the place B was in residency with about five other people we knew, more or less, and it was an impressive homecoming. They were all sitting around in the living room, rolling the day's first joint, and watching *Green Acres* on the tube.

"Great show...great show," somebody said. "But you have to do your head to appreciate it."

Green Acres of all things. A sit-com about city people on a farm. Welcome back to whatever was going to have to pass for the new 'real world.'

We only stayed in the Iron City for three or four days. One major thing I wanted to do was talk to my high school sweetheart, Debbie Milo. Gentle reader, a quick confession: the second week on the farm I had called Debbie to tell her that it would be better if she went off to her first year of college in the fall unattached. I was afraid to mention that phone call before this because it was an act of such colossal stupidity—she was intelligent, sweet and beautiful—that you would have no doubt thrown this Tall Tale against the wall in disgust over my later whining about the lack of a girlfriend. For some reason yet unclear, after spending freshman year at Williams in an often-difficult long distance love affair, I felt a need to be free of it for the summer ahead. Well, we have all seen how that worked out. Anyway, I wanted to see her and try to explain it was nothing she had done or not done, it just seemed like the right thing to do at the time. Naturally when we saw each other at a party that night all I wanted to do was take her in my arms, but she was wise enough to realize everything had changed and it was better to leave it at that.

On a brighter note, at least one of our old friends was paying attention to current events and lined up some entertainment for our brief visit to Pittsburgh. There was going to be an outdoor concert that weekend sponsored by the local AM radio station and proudly featuring four or five 'Bubble Gum' acts—their own marketing slogan, for Christ's sake—including the wretched monsters responsible for *Yummy Yummy Yummy, I've Got Love in my Tummy* (the Ohio Express, I think), and Archie Bell and the Drells. This was too good to miss, so an eager contingent loaded up on Budweiser quarts and threw down some blankets on a nice grassy hillside in a quiet city park. We were minus George though. My companion for that entire incredible summer missed the show. He was lying in a miserable heap in Dave Helwig's basement suffering through the worst case of Trench Mouth the world has ever seen. This disease not only sounds nasty, it is nasty. It is an unkind bug that ruins the inside of your mouth and throat for several days and you don't want to hear any more about it.[27]

---

27. Mrs. Helwig certainly didn't, but she apparently caught it after we left. I only learned of this catastrophe later that year when I tried to contact Dave during a vacation and she answered the phone. When I asked to talk to him she screamed something horrible at me and slammed down the receiver. Eventually I got a hold of him at Yale and asked what in God's name I had done to piss off his mother, and he explained that she hated George and me with an overwhelming passion and never wanted to see us again. George ran into the same thing before I had a chance to warn him. She was really going crazy when David's father Gilbert, a delightful man, evidently snatched the phone away from her and apologized. "You have to understand the intensity of the feelings here," he said. That's how nasty trench mouth is.

The announcer, who gave new meaning to the term 'jive-ass disc jockey,' kept insisting to the few hundred people there that "This is just like Woodstock!" to the delight of the Mount Lebanon crew. As recent veterans of the real thing, George and my stock was floating pretty high amongst our old friends just then, so a casual quizzical tilt of my head in response to those announcements was enough to quietly mock his strange, forced enthusiasm. Hell, we all felt like Strangers in a Strange Land at a concert like this. Much of the rest of the relatively small crowd in attendance seemed to be taking the 'Bubble Gum' show in a fine spirit of irony as well, booing loudly through Yummy Yummy and other insults. The afternoon's high (or low) point came, sadly enough, at the expense of the Drells.

In my years of playing music I have witnessed many horrors, from your basic equipment malfunction to hostile and even dangerous audiences. Twelve nights in a Hells Angels' bar in Redwood City, California comes to mind. Fuck an innocent Duck. But the worst thing that can happen is a total band melt-down on stage. These are both rare and unforgettable. In fact, the more carefully rehearsed you are, the more intricate the arrangement of an original tune, the more you leave yourselves open to this possibility. The heaviest adult dose of that I ever experienced was with a band called Evening Stage George and I later put together in L.A. We rehearsed constantly and performed almost always for free, auditioning occasionally in famous clubs like the Troubadour and the Whiskey. One evening in some stinking bar somewhere in that vast nest of vipers known as Orange County, the wheels came off and for many agonizing measures all five members of the band were completely lost. We might as well have been playing with Ravi Shankar.

One of the singer/song writers in the group, a beautiful human being named Joe Celura, later said that it felt like a great hole had suddenly opened up in the stage and we were all being swallowed by it. That's exactly what it seemed like to me, but at least we didn't come to a complete stop. As a drummer, I knew instinctively to keep playing; just plow on as if everything is fine and hope that somehow the others will rally around you. I don't know what kind of bad dreams you have, but mine are filled with moments like that (Where oh Where is the God Damned Down Beat!?) and with drum sets that dissolve and mutate or are even set up backwards facing away from the audience. Long ago, however, I realized that these are very useful exercises sent by the gods to allow you to laugh off the horrible things that actually do go wrong when you are playing while wide awake.[28]

You know, digressions are all well and good—(have you been reading the footnotes?)—but we have left poor Archie back on that stage in Pittsburgh long enough. I suppose it's alright, because no matter what we say or do here, if those sorry bastards are still alive, they have recurring nightmares about that beautiful sunny afternoon in 1969 and are beyond our help.

---

28.   Want to hear another savage example? July 3rd, Placitas, New Mexico, 1978—big out-door stage at a festival. Our country rock band, Boarding House Reach, has just started the second song of the set when the lead guitar player on my right, Mark Karen, turns and begins frantically signaling me to slow down the tempo. At the same moment, George, playing bass on my left, starts screaming at me to pick it up. They are both tripping on acid...I am not. My vast experience in Dreamland Drummer Hell allows me not to panic and to realize that the groove we are in must be just about right, and so I smile and nod in agreement at both of them and keep the song going right where it is.

The Tighten Up, their signature song, had two things going for it: an infectious beat and that magic moment at the beginning when Archie yells into the mic, "Hi Everybody! I'm Archie Bell and the Drells from Houston Texas! We not only Sing! But we can Dance just as Good as We Walk!" We were all waiting to hear this live, hell the whole crowd was. These Brothers were the only more-or-less real band on the program that day and the audience was primed. The Drells came out and started playing the groove, building towards Archie's dramatic opening. The only problem was that whatever half-assed P.A. the promoters had slapped together for their Bubble Gum Extravaganza picked that exact moment to take a crap. Poor Archie grabbed the microphone and nothing came out. Nothing. The band played bravely on.... and on...but no one could make that dead mic come to life, and so Archie danced pathetically around for awhile looking like a headliner who has just lost his head. Eventually the song petered out and they all just gave up and walked off the stage. It was a perfectly fitting end to that sorry excuse for a rock concert but I felt bad for the Drells. We were left lying there on those blankets in the sun quietly sipping our beers and laughing at the little jokes the universe seems to delight in playing on people when they least expect it.

chapter sixteen

Not much left to tell. Although this has been (as advertised) a Tall Tale filled with larger than life characters and improbable events, it should be noted here, near the end, that everything in this story really happened. Sure, some of the dialogue has been reconstructed—my memory is not really that good—but the important words are real. Could you ever forget hearing a line like "Cows! First cows I've seen all day"? Or: "Ever hear of war?" I hope not.

At the end of the summer, all of the Heroes went their own separate ways. Guzzy, John V.B., Clarke and Mountain off to their different colleges, and George and I back to ours. I took my new-found-burned-ass-of-cow-hay-bale body and joined the rugby club at Williams that fall. George got a hot band together called Special Care (from a Buffalo-Springfield song) and started playing Harvard mixers and girls' schools around Boston.

We did get the crew together again during winter break early the next year and it was memorable. Somebody's family—best guess: the Sanford's—owned a cabin in the woods somewhere and about fifteen people made a stand there for three or four days. You couldn't drive all the way up to it because it was full winter in the Catskills, so everything and everybody got hauled up by snowmobile. Kegs were expertly lashed onto childhood sleds, for instance, and pulled merrily along through the snow. It was a fine reunion, complete with the making of new friends and the kissing of the occasional young lady. My favorite memories involve screaming around a small lake just below the cabin on those snowmobiles and converting an old rocking chair into a 'sit-up' sled by knocking off the rockers and attaching straight boards on to the legs. This simple adjustment allowed you to go barrel-assing down a steep slope and out on the lake while still maintaining a tight grip upon your Beveridge of Choice. Don't try this at home.

One of the conference attendees I had not met before was a giant red-haired guy named Dwayne who supplied a lot of unintentional entertainment during the long weekend. He was famous for maintaining a Drewish capacity for fucking up nearly everything he touched. The boys introduced him as 'Dopey Dwayne' and it was easy to see how he had earned that particular term of endearment. Unlike Drew, however, who was arrogant enough to take a good man's sports car for a joy ride without asking, the big boy was on the quiet side and seemed to be compassionate. I liked him immediately. Sometime Saturday afternoon he began doing Bear-like orbits of the area, both indoors and outside and eventually I asked Guzzy what that might be about.

"Oh, the dopey bastard lost one of his front teeth...you know, one of those fake ones? He thinks he's going to find it."

At one point the next day I found him methodically ripping up the two or three old wooden steps leading into the cabin. "Pretty sure it's under here," he was muttering to himself while he worked. You may find this hard to swallow, but people in Margaretville swear to this day that Dwayne caused the infamous near-melt down at Three Mile Island in Pennsylvania some years later. He was certainly working there, and I have no trouble at all believing the story.

The other lasting image seared into my brain was waking up the final morning in the soft pre-dawn light, sitting on the floor with my back to one of the walls of what passed for a living room. Taking stock of the situation, I noticed Clarke about ten feet away, camped at the foot of the back-up keg we had gone all the way to Kingston the afternoon before to procure. Realizing I was awake, he nodded, reached up, slowly poured himself a cup full and took a nice long drink. Smiling that wonderful smile of his, he said confidently:

"This beer has a certain drinkability."

That pretty much covers our adventures in the mud and the blood and the beer in that far away time. But what of the 'True Love' that was promised at the beginning of this story? Well...every Tall Tale needs at least one giant whopper and this was it. True love may happen ("as you wish"), but it was not to be for George and Claire. The true part is that they were in love that summer—they certainly were genuinely happy together, which admittedly was not often—but the romance did not survive much beyond autumn. Sorry about not providing exciting details of love making in the barn etc. This was something I was not invited to and it didn't happen anyway as far as I know. Boy, they kissed a lot, but that was their business and not ours.

My brother and I somehow managed to make it through those Ivy League colleges. There didn't seem to be any reason to attempt graduate school when we "matriculated" because our shared draft number, '69'!! − was a winner in the first Vietnam lottery and threatened to matriculate us into a body bag. This was a fate we spent a year desperately trying to avoid, until old Ricky Nixon finally found that elusive light at the end of the tunnel and called the whole thing off.

For that year, we rented a house in Aaaahhhlington Heights outside of Boston and kept Special Care alive with a 50/50 roster of Williams and Harvard musicians. The band was managed by our once and future friend, Ty Cobb, who had a delightful habit of showing up for tri-weekly poker games dressed like Bret Maverick, Colt Forty-five and all. The Kansas boy proved to be an apt manager. In a phone call to a college president who had shorted us after a gig, he once said, "Look Mr. I'm tired of dealing with a senile mind fogged with greed." We got the money.

The summer of '73 was spent in Detroit working as live-in janitors in a gigantic old Baptist church by day and rehearsing a new band, doing only original material, in the choir room at night. Then we purchased an old Wonder Bread truck in Port Huron, Michigan for $50 and aimed it west towards California and dreams of rock and roll glory, arriving in L.A. with something like $1.86 left between five of us. But those are all Tall Tales for some other time.

George is out in northern California near our brother Larry, still writing and playing that extraordinary music which comes directly from his generous heart out into the world. Mountain ran a state park in Illinois for twenty- five years. No point in trying to civilize that beautiful rascal any further. John V.B. has been a college professor, teaching environmental science, and Clarke taught college as well, out in California. Guzzy became the top-kick of a crew laying down runways and other massive stretches of asphalt down towards New York City. Three of us—Guz, Clarke and myself—after living in several different far-flung places, now call the Catskills our home. These mountains finally called us back.

Roland and Faye continued to work the farm for many years with an assortment of hired hands, finally managing to sell their herd for a good price before the family dairy farm business went completely belly up in this part of New York State. Rol was busy raising three heifers and tooling about on tractors until just before his death in early June of 1998, a few weeks before haying fever would have kicked in. Our dear Faye lived on there with her son for many more years, and as Andy recently said, "she was still a pisser right to the end."

I was sitting with them one Sunday afternoon in that sweet old living room (which had not changed all that much since the days of the Gram blanket) watching the television news broadcasting images of New Orleans during Hurricane Katrina.[29] George Bush suddenly appeared, shirt sleeves carefully rolled up, sporting his smug Yale-frat-boy smile. Faye, then in her early nineties, got up out of Roland's favorite armchair and pointed at the screen.

"Look at him! He was born into so much money he has no idea what these poor people are going through! What an asshole!"

Then she glanced shyly at the two of us and said, "I'm sorry boys, he just makes me so mad."

Faye died in August of 2014. She and Roland, my two parents from the summer of '69, are buried in the little cemetery just outside the village of New Kingston next to Gram.

---

29. One real difference was the air quality. It no longer smelled so distinctly of cow shit—more like your over-heated grandmother's house. I must admit, though, after all of these years, that I grew to like the original version a good deal more.

It is a beautiful place and I visit it from time to time to stand near them and reflect upon how lucky we have been to get to know such amazing people.

A few years before Roland died, I was visiting the farm and he said, "Come on John, let's take a ride." So we got into his old pick-up truck and he drove down the valley somewhere near where the Butler Brothers' farm used to be, and turned off on a little dirt road that follows the course of the river for a ways. It is called Johnny Cake Lane. When he showed me the road sign, he got that old mischievous Boss twinkle in his eyes and chuckled softly.

"I thought you might want to see this place," he said.

He was right.

> So I'll ply the fire with kindling,
> And pull the blankets to my chin.
> I'll lock the vagrant winter out
> And bolt my wanderin' in.
> I'd like to call back summertime
> And have her stay for just another month or so..
> But she's got the urge for going,
> And I guess she's bound to go.
>   Joni Mitchell

appendix A and B

(Any book with footnotes ought to have an appendix)

A. A few years before she died, the Reverends Harter helped to publish a collection of Laura Van Benschoten's (Gram's) poetry "as part of the New Kingston Valley Community Whoop-De-Doo." (Yes, there really is such a thing.) The booklet is titled: *Poems of the Catskills*, and features a beautiful introduction by her grandson Andy. It contains twenty-nine poems by Gram, ending with one by her mother, Harriett Beckwith Worden, written in 1885. This is the third one in the collection; she named it "Calling the Cows." I remember Roland using the expression "Co-Boss" in just this way. Who knows how old that is.

Time to call the cows, boys,
They wander far away.
This is what we do, boys,

    At the close of every day.
    Co-Boss, Co-Boss, Co-Boss
       Here Rufus, Here Rufus

The boys are from the city.
They find there's not much play.
We have to get the cows, boys,
At the close of every day.

    Co-Boss, Co-Boss, Co-Boss
       Here Rufus, Here Rufus

Then early in the morning
Before the break of day
Get the cows down from the pasture.
"No easy life," they say.

    Co-Boss, Co-Boss, Co-Boss
       Here Rufus, Here Rufus

Later in the evening
When all the chores are done,
They will find a way to get to town,
And then they will have some fun.

    Co-Boss, Co-Boss, Co-Boss
       Here Rufus, Here Rufus

    1973

Written for the Kincheloe boys in Hollywood.
They thought getting the cows was hard work.

B.   In the late 90's, I was standing in my kitchen in the little village of Halcottsville one evening when Billy Finch, a young friend of ours, came staggering in pretty drunk with an equally drunk friend he wanted to introduce. His name was John Van Benschoten. Whaugh. He was a big handsome guy from a branch of the V.B's I didn't know about. I figured out later that he's related to Roland by his great grandfather Jay being a first cousin to Andrew V.B., Roland's dad. Now that's complicated. We were complete strangers to each other but hit it off immediately. At that time he was living in the New Kingston valley with his brother on a farm and working it part time. Somehow we got to talking about music and this young Van Benschoten, who turns out to be a wonderful musician, allowed as how he had just finished working on an original song using words from a poem an elderly relative had written long ago called "Calling the Cows."

"That's very nice," I said, laughing. "Your new song is about me."

Strange planet we have here.